Penguin Education SH 4

Britain and the World
1789-1901

A. M. Newth

Mrs A. M. Newth was educated at Haberdashers' Aske's School, Acton, and spent a year in Germany including a term at the University of Munich, before reading for the History Tripos at Newnham College, Cambridge. She taught for several years in a girls' high school and later in a boys' grammar school, where she was Head of the History Department.

A History of Britain

SH 1   Out of the Ancient World

SH 2   Medieval and Tudor Britain

SH 3   The Making of a Nation 1603–1789

SH 4   Britain and the World 1789–1901

SH 5   Britain in the Modern World: the Twentieth Century

Britain and the World 1789-1901

A. M. Newth

Penguin Books

Design: Arthur Lockwood

Illustration research: Enid Moore, Rosemary Barnicoat

Penguin Books Ltd, Harmondsworth, Middlesex, England
Penguin Books Inc., 3300 Clipper Mill Road, Baltimore, Md 21211, U.S.A.
Penguin Books Australia Ltd, Ringwood, Victoria, Australia

First published 1967, reprinted with corrections 1968, 1969
Copyright © A. M. Newth, 1967

Printed in Great Britain, web offset, by Hazells Offset Ltd, Leigh Road, Slough, Bucks
Set in Lumitype Plantin

This book is sold subject to the condition that it shall not, by way of trade or otherwise, be
lent, re-sold, hired out, or otherwise circulated without the publisher's prior consent in any
form of binding or cover other than that in which it is published and without a similar
condition including this condition being imposed on the subsequent purchaser

Contents

Chapter 1   England during the French wars   1789–1815   *page* 6

Chapter 2   After the wars   28

Chapter 3   After the Reform Bill   1832–34   42

Chapter 4   England   1834   60

Chapter 5   The royal family and foreign affairs   1848–65   72

Chapter 6   Railways and the Great Exhibition   84

Chapter 7   Politics   1867–1900   100

Chapter 8   Ireland   124

Chapter 9   Town and village life   136

Chapter 10   Science, inventions and education   160

Chapter 11   You and the doctor   180

Chapter 12   The British Empire   194

Index   219

Acknowledgements   223

Chapter 1
England during the French wars 1789-1815

The regular troops held for the protection of Paris were persuaded to join the people; they were encamped in the Champs de Mars to the number of five thousand men and marched to the Hotel of Invalids, a building on the outskirts of the city; the Invalids joined the rest and brought away all the great guns and other ammunition belonging to the Hospital. With this reinforcement the people then attacked the Bastille prison, which they soon made themselves master of, and released all the state prisoners there. *The Times – 20 July 1789*

There are people alive whose great-great-grandparents read this in their newspapers. But why, when we are writing about England, should we begin with something which happened in France? Sometimes events in one country can have tremendous effects on other countries, and the French Revolution altered not only the history of France, but that of all the other nations in Europe.

The French Revolution

In 1788 Louis XVI, the King of France, was told by his ministers that there was no more money in the Treasury; the government was bankrupt. Yet France was a rich country; it produced finer silks, porcelain, furniture, and jewellery than any other nation. It had, too, a large merchant navy, good ports and every possibility of growing rich by trade. In spite of all this the government could not find the money to carry on.

For 150 years France had been involved in expensive wars; enormous amounts had been spent on building royal palaces. Even so, the country might have stood the strain if the system of taxing the people had been different. The nobles, who were the richest people, had the privilege of not paying many taxes at all, so that most money had to come from the middle classes and the peasants. It was collected in such an inefficient way that only about half the amount ever reached the Treasury; the rest was lost to the tax collectors. Then the merchants suffered from high duties which they had to pay when they took their goods to the ports, so that trade began to decline. The peasants were even worse off, for they had to pay taxes to the state and also to their landlords.

Critics of the government

There were many intelligent men in France who saw that this system must lead to disaster, but they had no means by which they could put

Louis XVI.

6

Storming of the Bastille,
14 July 1789. The soldiers in
the middle are French Guards
who joined the mob in revolt.
The cannon which they
brought to help is causing the
billowing clouds of smoke.

their point of view or express their opinions. If anyone criticized the government he might find himself in prison for an indefinite period; nothing could be printed unless it had been passed by the censor; there was neither free speech nor free press. Louis XV had borrowed recklessly; his grandson Louis XVI was a well-meaning man who unfortunately had no understanding of the situation. When his ministers told him they could not borrow any more money or raise any more in taxation, they advised him to call together the States General, the Parliament in France.

The States General meets

There had been no meeting of the States General for more than 150 years. Excitement ran high, and on one point nearly everyone was agreed: the nobles must lose their privileges. Finally the delegates met at Versailles, which is about twelve miles from Paris. There were three

Houses in this Parliament: the House of Nobles, the House of Clergy, and the House of Commons. This last one, called the Third Estate, demanded that all three Houses should sit and vote together. They had a shrewd notion that the Nobles would cling to their privileges, but that if they were in one House they would be outvoted by the Commons. Louis hesitated; he got different advice from each minister he asked. Meanwhile the people in Paris were waiting impatiently to know what was being decided at Versailles. They knew that the unpopular Queen, Marie Antoinette, had sympathy with the nobles; they also knew that troops were being summoned to Versailles from the provinces. The troops might be turned against the city, where the people were ardent supporters of reform. When they heard that Louis had dismissed the popular minister, Necker, they waited no longer.

Meeting of the National Assembly in the covered tennis court at Versailles where members took an oath to give France a constitution. They were forced to meet in this unusual place when an order was given to close their usual hall.

Fall of the Bastille 1789

Determined to forestall any attack, on 14 July the people seized guns from the Invalides (a place where retired soldiers lived and where arms were stored) and stormed the fortress prison, the Bastille, which stood at the south-east of Paris, its guns trained on the Faubourg S. Antoine, the most thickly populated part of Paris. After a short but violent struggle the Governor gave up the keys; the people of Paris had won the day. When Louis XVI heard of it he is supposed to have said 'It is a revolt.' 'No Sire,' was the answer, 'it is a revolution.' It was in fact a turning point. Louis gave way to the demands of the Third Estate, the members of which now called themselves the 'National Assembly'. They invited the members of the House of Nobles to join them. When some of them had, Count Mirabeau became the leader of the Assembly. They took over the function of law making. All feudal privileges were abolished, all men were to be equal before the law, and trial by jury was introduced. Louis, whether he approved of this or not, had to sign these new decrees.

Why Britain went to war

When people in Britain read about the storming of the Bastille, many of them were horrified at the violence of the Paris mob, while others thought it a splendid thing that the French people were forcing their government to undertake reforms. After all, when the French were demanding free speech, trial by jury, and equality before the law, they were only asking for what the English already had. Some, however, like William Pitt, the Prime Minister, were hesitant. Other powers, particularly Austria and Prussia, whose governments were just as tyrannical as that of the old régime in France, grew alarmed lest these ideas spread over the frontiers of France like a disease. They sent threatening messages to the Assembly. But the French had tasted freedom, and when they realized that foreign armies were converging on their country, they hastily called for a citizen army. In 1792 with the tricolour flag and the motto 'Liberty, Equality, Fraternity', the French

This poster and others like it were put up on houses by the occupants to show their loyalty to the Republic. The two loyal citizens shown here are wearing the republican colours of white (the ancient colour of the flag of France) with red and blue (the colours of the city of Paris).

The death of Louis XVI. With him are his confessor, the Mayor of Paris, and the executioner, Santerre. This instrument was designed by Dr Guillotin for humane reasons. Its action was quicker than that of the clumsy axe.

marched against the two most powerful military states in Europe, Austria and Prussia. To the amazement of the world, after an initial setback, the French conquered South Germany and the Netherlands. In 1792 they declared the mouth of the Rhine, called the Scheldt, open to international commerce. This was a breach of an international agreement and Pitt thought it would injure our trade. He protested and France declared war on Great Britain. From 1793 until 1815, with only one short interval, England was at war.

Attitude of the people

There was popular support for the war at first. In 1792 the French had tried Louis XVI and Marie Antoinette for treason, guillotined them and set up a republic. Refugees poured into this country bringing with them tales of horror. Excited mobs attacked the houses of those whom they suspected of being sympathetic to the French. In Birmingham the house of the famous scientist, Dr Priestley, was burnt, his library and scientific instruments destroyed during three days' rioting, while the authorities stood idly by and did nothing to stop the attackers. Pitt and his Tory cabinet believed that talk of even the mildest kind of reform was dangerous. There were many societies which were interested in making the English Parliament more democratic by allowing more people to vote. Pitt himself had once been an advocate of what is called parliamentary reform, though he had never supported it very vigorously. Now, however, he felt the subject was dangerous. The leaders of a club called the London Corresponding Society were arrested and tried before a Middlesex jury, although they had done little more than press for a few much-needed reforms. When they were finally acquitted, after a long trial, Pitt suspended the Habeas Corpus Act, so that the Englishman's valued right of trial soon after imprisonment was withdrawn, and people could be kept in prison indefinitely. He also passed a law making it treason to criticize the constitution. The attitude of the authorities is shown clearly in Edinburgh, when Lord Braxfield, the Lord Justice Clerk, was trying a man called Gerard, who had attended a reform meeting. Gerard said that Jesus Christ had been a reformer; Braxfield's reply was 'Muckle he made of that. He was hangit.' When sentences of transportation for seven or fourteen years or for life would be given for such offences, only very courageous people would continue the struggle, so the movement for the reform of Parliament was postponed for thirty years.

Pitt's war policies

Pitt's conduct of the war and his financial policy were not entirely successful. He thought England's part in the war was to fight at sea and keep the ports open, while Austria and Prussia would fight on land. He raised large loans, thus increasing the National Debt, and lent money to the allies, who did not spend it all on the war effort. Finally he suspended cash payments from the Bank of England and issued more notes than could be met by the gold reserve. The effect of these measures was an increase of taxation and a sharp rise in prices, a rise which fell most heavily on the wage earners, whose wages did not rise to correspond with prices. The allies were a disappointment to us; Prussia made peace in 1795, Austria in 1797; then England was left to fight on her own until Austria entered the war again in 1799, only to come out again in 1801. We had to fight as far away as India, where the French stirred up rebellion against the East India Company. On the sea we were successful, defeating the French navy in the Mediterranean, and also defeating the Danish and Dutch navies which were used against us. The Danes objected to our searching their ships and the Dutch navy had been taken over by the French. We drove the French out of the West Indies, but the high death rate from fever made it a costly victory. We tried to support a royalist rising in Toulon, but were driven out by Napoleon. Admiral Howe defeated the French fleet off Brest, a battle which is always called the 'glorious first of June'. The object of the attack had been to prevent the ships bringing corn to France from getting into port, and the glory of the victory was dimmed when it was learned that the shipments had got through.

Effect of the war on industry

Pitt had entered the war for the sake of English trade and commerce. The merchants wanted the trade routes, now threatened by the

A sketch made by the artist, David, of Marie Antoinette as she was being driven to the guillotine.

French, kept open. But it was not the manufacturers and merchants themselves who fought the war; the actual fighting was done by the soldiers and sailors, and the materials needed to carry on the war were made by the English workers. You would naturally expect that those who bore the brunt of the work should share in the gains it might bring. It did not happen like that. The war brought a big increase in trade and was what is called a 'stimulus to production' because we needed equipment for our armed forces. The process of turning to steam power was speeded up. It is easy to see why this happened. A manufacturer might have been making quite a good income by using domestic labour, or water power; he might therefore hesitate before investing in an expensive machine when he was not certain there would be either enough raw material or a big enough market to justify the cost. A war means government orders. Then in 1793 the cotton gin (a machine for getting the seeds out of the raw cotton) was invented in America, and after that the supply of raw cotton was rapidly increased. In 1760 we had imported from America 3 million pounds. At the end of 1800 we were importing 56 million pounds. It was cheap and all the world wanted cheap clothing, and Lancashire set out to supply the world. No wonder the Lancashire mill-owners favoured the war which kept the trade routes open. Yorkshire was slower to turn to steam because the supply of wool was then limited to what could be produced in England.

Effects of machinery on the working population

More men were needed to make the machines, but fewer men were needed to work them. There was a greater proportion of women and children working in the new mills because they were cheaper. If the local supply of children was not enough, the authorities sent pauper apprentices from London. According to a law dating from Queen Elizabeth's reign, the parish must apprentice the pauper children; this could now be done quite cheaply by sending the children north

Starving children stealing food from a pig's trough. The illustration, called 'Children of the Poor', comes from a book called *The Life and Adventures of Michael Armstrong* written by Frances Trollope in 1840, to arouse the conscience of the rich.

where they were handed over to a mill-owner. In a situation like this what could the men do? They saw their work taken over by women and children, and their own wages lowered, this at a time when prices were rising owing to the war. Their first response was to join together to defend their standard of living. This idea of association was an old one. There had always been Friendly Societies of handloom weavers and spinners; they had been formed to help the members who were ill or in trouble. The object of a manufacturer is to make a profit; and the lower his wages bill, the greater the profit. When there were twenty men and only one job, the employer could pay the lowest wage which any one of the men would take. By combining in a union the men thought they would be able to bargain for higher wages. Then complaints were sent to the Cabinet by the employers saying that the practice of forming unions was harmful to trade. The government acted promptly, and in 1799 and 1800 passed two laws forbidding any combination of persons who designed to interfere with trade. They were always known as the combination laws. Trade unions after this could only carry on in secret.

The Luddite movement

Is it any wonder that the textile workers saw Parliament as an enemy and not as a protector? There was the harsh law which tore men from their homes and sent them to Australia for such actions as joining their fellows in trying to get a living wage. When men see the law as an instrument of injustice they become lawless. Several years after the combination laws had been passed there was a trade depression, made worse in Nottinghamshire and in Yorkshire by two new inventions. In Nottingham most of the people earned their living making stockings on a stocking frame in their own homes. When the manufacturers found they could do this more cheaply on a machine, riots broke out, led by the men who had become unemployed, and machines were wrecked. These riots are always known as the Luddite riots, because there was a popular rumour that they were organized by someone called Ned Ludd. Soldiers were brought in to protect the factories.

In Yorkshire, in the West Riding, there were people called 'croppers' who cut the nap off the cloth. They too found they were left idle when machines were installed to do this work of finishing the cloth. The mill-owners appealed to Parliament for troops, and had men on guard all night at their factories. A certain Mr Cartwright had a mill near Liversedge, which was attacked one night by about 200 men armed with guns, pistols, stakes and hammers. He had several soldiers with him, to ward off the attack, and in a letter he wrote to the Home Office he says 'The assailants being driven back we found they had left behind them two men mortally wounded, who however from untoward circumstances made no disclosure of their associates.' He does not explain what those 'untoward circumstances' were; the men and women of the neighbourhood could have given a more complete account. The two

Rawford's Mill in Yorkshire where Luddites broke in and wrecked machines.

men were Booth, a lad of nineteen, the son of a local clergyman, and Hartley, a former worker at Mr Cartwright's mill, aged twenty-four. They lay bleeding in the courtyard of the mill and Mr Cartwright forbade anyone to touch them until they gave him the names of the leaders. In the morning when a crowd gathered, Cartwright was obliged, because of the anger of the onlookers, to allow someone to carry them into a house and summon a doctor. A clergyman, Mr Robertson, went with them, hung over the suffering men and urged them to disclose the names of the leaders. At last Booth raised his head. 'Can you keep a secret?' he asked. 'I can,' replied the clergyman eagerly, as he bent forward to catch the names. 'So can I,' answered Booth, who soon after died. Hartley died the following morning.

The Luddite movement was bound to fail. Once a quicker and cheaper method of manufacture has been discovered it is impossible to prevent its being used. These riots left behind great bitterness. The mill-owners were ruthless because they stood to lose their mills and their whole livelihood as a result of armed attacks. When trade revived these troubles died down, though the fear of them remained for a long time.

Effect of the war on the rural areas

The war brought employment to the countryside. Food was needed because of the difficulty of importing corn. This meant that all available land was used. Marginal land, that is land on which it was possible to grow crops, though not fertile enough to make it worth the labour, was now brought into cultivation. The price of corn rose, so that the big farmers made big profits. The landowners shared in the prosperity; they could and did demand higher rents. When a lease of land fell in, it could be renewed for a bigger rent. Dear bread made the landowner and farmer fat. It kept the labourer poor and half-starved. He had lost by this time – except in a very few villages – his rights of common, and had only his wages to rely on and those remained the same even though the cost of food rose. For him to join a union was almost impossible. In a village there could be no secrets; no activity could be concealed. The standard of living of the farm labourers went down.

The navy

Some of the younger and stronger men might enlist in the army or the navy. As the war progressed the need for men grew, particularly in the navy. Vigorous use was made of the press gangs, that terror of wives and mothers. Unsuspecting youths might be lured into accepting the King's shilling, or simply spirited away. When James Watt, the inventor, was living in London for three years he did not set foot on the pavement, he was so afraid of the press gang. Here is an account by Robert Hay, whose ship was lying at anchor at Bristol. It was a merchant ship. Men preferred this service to the navy, because of better pay and better conditions. The gangs were not supposed to take skilled men off a merchant ship, but they would take anyone when short of men.

14

A press gang at work.

I was a few steps up the fore rigging when I heard one of the boys calling in an Irish whisper, 'Carpenter, carpenter, down, down, the gang are alongside.' A moment found me on deck hurrying to the after hatchway. Ere I could reach it I found myself seized by the arm. I trembled. 'You are running right on them,' whispered the boy, who had called me from the rigging, 'they are on the quarter-deck. Down, down, the forepeak or you are gone.' I darted like lightning and in a twinkling found myself between two tiers of sugar sacks, trembling like a leaf. In a minute or two several of the gang came down the forepeak to search. 'I can see you, my old genius,' said one, 'and I can see you, my fine fellow,' said another. 'You may as well come out quietly,' said a third, 'for out you shall come.' 'Hand yourself over here at once,' vociferated a rough, appalling voice, 'or the cutlass will taste your beef in a jiffy.' And on this they began to thrust their cutlasses down to the hilt in the interstices of the sugar sacks. Happily I was more than a cutlass length down, and I took special care to let them have all the talking to themselves, and to breathe softly. After waiting half an hour I heard the voice of my former warner calling out that the gang had gone.

Conditions in the navy

Small wonder that they found it difficult to man the King's ships. Crowded down in cramped quarters (fourteen inches to each man's hammock), badly fed, often cheated of their wages, and often brutally ill-treated, the seamen on whom Britain relied to guard her shores had little reward for their valour. It is true there was the prospect of prize money. If an enemy ship was taken, part of the value was divided amongst the crew. Apart from this there was nothing much to attract men to join the navy. Boys who gave way to the romantic idea of running away to sea generally regretted it after a short dose of a seaman's life. Petitions were sent to the Admiralty from some of the ships. They tell their own story.

Draft us on board any of His Majesty's ships, as we don't wish to go to sea in the *Winchelsea* . . . our usage was more like Turks than that of British seamen . . . we are knocked about so that we do not know what to do. Every man of her would sooner be shot at like a taregaite by musketree than remain any longer in her . . . the ill-treatment which we do receive from the tiriant of a captain from time to time, which is more than the spirits of man can bear. For we were born free and now we are slaves . . . we hope your Lordships will grant us a new commander or a new ship for our captain is one of the most barbarous and most inhuman officers an unfortunate set of men had the misfortune to be with.

Not all officers were brutal. This story is told of Admiral Collingwood by one of the men on his ship:

He was walking the quarter-deck one very cold day, when a maintop man with a jacket through which the wind had free ingress mounted the Jacob's ladder.
'Where are you going, my lad?' asked the Admiral.
'To the lookout on the masthead, your Honour.'
'Have you no warmer jacket than that to put on?'
'I have no other, your Honour, but my mustering one.'
'Jacobs,' said he to the signal man, 'tell my coxswain to come here.'
'How many jackets have you, Davis?'
'Four, your Honour.'
'Jump down and bring the second-best one here, and if you have a spare leg of trouser lying by, put it in one of the pockets.' Davis's second-best jacket soon covered the shoulders of the maintop man.
'Remind me of this when we go ashore, Davis.'
    There was no need to remind him and I need hardly say that Davis was not out of pocket by this transaction.

Mutiny at Spithead   1797

It is not surprising that the seamen used to petition to sail with Admiral Collingwood, or Admiral Howe, (Black Dick, as he was affectionately called) or other officers, such as Nelson, who were humane as well as capable. But these men were the exceptions; the majority of seamen could expect little but harsh treatment. Yet the English people were proud of their navy and its traditions; they relied on it as they did on the Bank of England, something which protected them and kept them safe. It came like the clap of a thunderbolt when they learnt that on Easter Sunday morning 1797, after an order had been given to weigh anchor at Spithead, not a movement was seen. The ships lay idle. It

Nelson's Flag Ship, the
Victory. It was launched in
1765 but re-fitted for Nelson
in 1801. It carried 102 guns
and was 226 feet long.

Cartoon of a sailor praying
that 'the enemies' shot may be
distributed in the same
proportion as the prize money,
the greatest part among the
officers!'

was more like a strike than a mutiny, because we always connect fighting and bloodshed with a mutiny. This was orderly, calm and disciplined. The Lords of the Admiralty, shocked out of their slumbers, immediately thought the men had treasonable ideas borrowed from the French. Here they were quite wrong, as they found out when they hurried down to investigate. There was no doubt of the seamen's loyalty. 'If the French put out from Brest, we will go at them and beat them,' they declared. Their complaints were simple; they wanted better food, better pay, and shore leave, and the right to petition. The sailors' pay had not been increased since the time of Cromwell; an ordinary seaman had 19s. a month; after deductions it might be only 10s. The question of shore leave was a burning one. Often after months at sea the men were not allowed to leave the ship when it docked, for fear of desertions. After delay and muddle, discussions and suggestions, the mutiny was settled largely by the common sense of Admiral Howe, who interviewed all the delegates from the ships. The final result was that the seamen gained all their demands and a pardon from the King. Howe dismissed fifty-nine officers who had been proved unworthy. This, more than anything else, convinced the men of the sincerity of the Admiralty. A month later a more contented fleet sailed away from Spithead.

Rise of Napoleon

All the time we were fighting France, it was becoming a different kind of war, because France itself was changing. In 1793 we had gone to war against a revolutionary country which had set out to bring freedom to its neighbours. The middle classes in France had made great gains; they had got rid of all the restrictions on trade which had hampered them. They now wanted to halt the movement. For them it had gone far enough. They skilfully got rid of the old leaders and put in power a small committee of five men, called the Directory. In doing this they were helped by a clever young Captain of Artillery, Napoleon Bonaparte. He first cleared the streets of Paris for them, then he led the army into Italy where he defeated the Austrians in 1797. What his plans were after that we do not know; it is generally assumed that he intended to go far east. Anyway, he got as far as Egypt. There he was cut off from his supplies when the French fleet was defeated by the British fleet at the Battle of the Nile. Napoleon managed to return to Italy, escaping his British pursuers. He defeated the Austrians (who had taken to arms again), returned to Paris, where he ousted the Directory and made himself Consul, so that by 1800 we were not fighting a France which believed in Liberty, Equality, and Fraternity, but a France governed by Napoleon. But for the Revolution, Napoleon would never have had his chance; he came from an insignificant family in Corsica. In 1804 he took the title of Emperor.

Reasons for Napoleon's success

He had little use for liberty; he himself would give the people good

Portrait of Napoleon from a medallion. His wreath of laurels is imitated from similar portraits of Roman emperors.

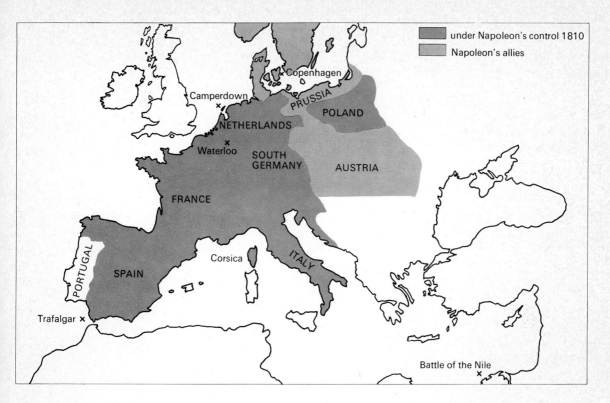

Map legend:
- under Napoleon's control 1810
- Napoleon's allies

Map labels: Copenhagen, Camperdown ×, PRUSSIA, POLAND, NETHERLANDS, Waterloo ×, SOUTH GERMANY, AUSTRIA, FRANCE, PORTUGAL, SPAIN, Corsica, ITALY, Trafalgar ×, Battle of the Nile ×

By 1810, most of Europe was either allied to Napoleon or under his control.

government and make the laws. He believed in equality of opportunity, and promoted his officers only when they showed ability; one of his marshals was the son of an innkeeper, another the son of a cooper. That was the one idea of the Revolution which was of use to him. Anyone who looks at the list of Napoleon's victories might wonder how it was possible for him to have so many. One reason was that he was fighting old-fashioned aristocratic armies, whilst he used all the inventions of French technicians. The great scientist Fourier accompanied him to Egypt; the mathematicians Monge and Laplace were his advisers. He was professional in the modern sense of the term, while often his enemies fought with out-of-date methods.

In 1802 he made himself Consul for life. His armies controlled Italy, the Netherlands and South Germany. Only at sea was France not supreme. Our victory at the Battle of the Nile had foiled his plans in Egypt and when the Dutch and Danish fleets had been turned against England, they had been defeated at the Battles of Camperdown and Copenhagen.

If he was to defeat England, he must make careful preparations. He wanted a breathing space. So did Pitt. In 1802 they signed the Peace of Amiens.

The war at sea, Trafalgar   1805

Pitt could look at the first nine years of the war with little satisfaction, apart from the fact that we had consistently defeated the French at sea. There was unrest at home about the heavy taxation; money had been wasted on allies who had retired from the war; besides the mutiny at Spithead, there had been a rebellion in Ireland in 1798, and only a violent storm at sea had prevented the French from landing there. Pitt managed to get together another coalition against Napoleon when Austria joined with England in 1805, and war broke out again. Napoleon's aim was to smash England by invading with his army. It was at this period that those round Martello towers you see on the south coast were built to keep out the French.

Napoleon knew he must somehow lure the British fleet away from the Channel before he could land. The French began an attack in the West Indies, an attack which drew Nelson away to the west. Then, hearing of the French plans, he hurried back, intercepted the French fleet off Cape Trafalgar and inflicted a heavy defeat on them.

Death of Nelson. He is lying towards the right, collapsed on the deck, surrounded by officers.

Tragically, Nelson, one of our best naval commanders, lost his life in the battle. This was a decisive battle in the war at sea. So many ships were destroyed that Napoleon reckoned it would take five years to build up another large fleet, so he had to attack England in some other way.

Pitt died in 1806. It was said that his death was caused by the heart-breaking news that Napoleon had defeated the Austrians at the Battle of Austerlitz.

France attacks Britain's trade

Having failed to win at sea Napoleon thought of destroying Britain's trade. After defeating the Prussians (who had opposed French troops passing through their territory), he entered Berlin and issued the Berlin Decrees, which said that any country which traded with Britain would be counted as an enemy of France. Britain replied by the Orders in Council, which forbade the nations to trade with France. It was a question of which of the two countries could enforce their demands. Napoleon seemed invincible on land. He had one brother on the throne of Westphalia and another on the throne of Naples. In 1807, he tackled another European country, this time by negotiation; he met the Emperor Alexander of Russia on a barge in the River Niemen and signed the Treaty of Tilsit. By this treaty Alexander agreed to support Napoleon against Britain and in return he was to have a free hand in Finland, a country he conquered in 1808.

Napoleon's position may seem to have been a dazzling one. But he could not control all this territory without a vast army and without huge expenditure. His wars cost money and that money was largely drawn, not from France, but from the lands he had conquered. People who at first had welcomed many of the Emperor's reforms, now began to groan under the burden of his taxation. The Berlin Decrees proved a boomerang. Europeans wanted to buy British goods. There was always a good deal of smuggling, so that although British trade was damaged by the Decrees, it was not so seriously hurt as Napoleon had hoped it would be.

Wellington, by the Spanish painter Francisco Goya.

The Peninsular War

Then Portugal declared she would not agree to the Berlin Decrees. She had an Atlantic coastline and so could be protected by the British navy. Napoleon had no intention of letting the Peninsula (that is Spain and Portugal) fall into British hands. He forced the King of Spain to abdicate, put his brother Joseph from Naples on the throne and sent in French troops. This gave England an opportunity. We could transport men and munitions by sea, and British troops were landed in Portugal. The first commander, Sir John Moore, was killed in battle. Afterwards our army was commanded by Sir Arthur Wellesley (later made the Duke of Wellington). He was a brilliant general. At a time when people had begun to think that Napoleon's armies were invincible, Wellington proved that the French could be

defeated. He drove the French armies northward from Madrid and cleared them all out of Spain. This war was an added drain on the French resources and Napoleon referred to it as 'the Spanish ulcer'.

One of a series of etchings called 'The disasters of war' in which Goya described the brutality of war.

The Russian Campaign   1812

Napoleon had other difficulties. Russia began to object to keeping the terms of the Berlin Decrees. Napoleon called up 600,000 men and prepared to march into Russia, confident that he could easily defeat the Tsarist army. So certain was he of a quick victory that his troops were only equipped with summer uniforms. They had a long march through Germany and Poland, and when they came to Russian soil they met with a kind of resistance they had never had before. The Russians deserted their villages and destroyed crops and foodstuffs, taking away their cattle with them. Only once did Napoleon meet the army. That was thirty miles from Moscow at Borodino, where he won a victory,

The French retreating over the Beresina after the disastrous Russian campaign.

but at a terrible price. Then he marched into Moscow, and found the city nearly empty. The nobles had gone, having taken all their valuables with them to their country houses. Someone, it was never discovered who, set fire to the town and destroyed many of the houses. Napoleon had to retreat. He went ahead with the swiftest horses available, whilst his wretched army had to begin the awful march back. They starved and froze in the terrible Russian winter. The peasants returned to attack them as they struggled forward. Many were drowned in crossing the River Beresina. Of the 30,000 cavalry, there were only one hundred left and the total number of soldiers who returned to French soil was 20,000, out of the 600,000 who had set out in the early summer of 1812.

The first exile

While Napoleon was in Russia, a new coalition had been formed

against him and he was defeated at the Battle of Leipzig. After this he abdicated and was exiled to the Island of Elba, a short distance from the coast of southern France.

The allies collected in Paris and began to prepare to settle the affairs of Europe. Even after the fearful slaughter of French citizens which had resulted from Napoleon's wars, he still could command loyalty. There was a whisper in Paris: 'The violets will return in the spring.' The violet was the Napoleonic emblem. In March 1815, Napoleon did escape and, with half a dozen companions, landed in Cannes. You can see the actual spot where he landed if you ever visit that town. The allies hastily got an army together and sent it south to meet the Emperor. It was led by Marshal Ney, a Frenchman who opposed the Napoleonic government. He promised to bring Napoleon back in a cage. The road on which Napoleon marched is still called the 'Route Napoleon' and there is a statue of him at the point

Battle of Waterloo. This is the scene on Mont St Jean where Wellington took up his station. The English troops are charging down the hill away from us and their standard can be seen on the right.

where he met Marshal Ney. When Ney saw his old commander, he found he could not bring himself to fight against him; all his old loyalty returned. He went over to the Emperor's side together with his men, so Napoleon returned not in a cage but at the head of an army.

The Hundred Days and Waterloo   1815

Napoleon had three months in Paris. He knew the allied armies would invade France. He did not wait for them. He collected an army and marched towards Brussels, where Wellington and the British were stationed. Everyone in England knew that a battle was to be fought and waited in fearful anxiety for news of it. Wellington had no illusions. He knew it would be a hard fight. Some of his best troops had been sent to Canada, and had been replaced by raw recruits. He had, however, the famous Guards, who fought magnificently. The two armies met near Brussels on the field of Waterloo. Towards the end of a day of desperate fighting the Prussians under Blücher arrived, and Napoleon was defeated.

The first news to reach England was that a great battle had been fought and lost. Six hours later carrier pigeons brought the account of the victory.

Napoleon was exiled to St Helena, from which island he could not escape, and here he lived the last six years of his life.

For twenty-two years we had been at war almost continuously. The 'ogre' Bonaparte was at last defeated and the English people could breathe safely. Many of them hardly remembered the time before the war. The face of the country had changed: oaks had been cut down to build the King's ships, and villages had been absorbed into smoky towns. Peace at last, and what sort of peace would it be for the disbanded soldiers and sailors who had fought for their country, and for the miners and mill-workers who had built up Britain's industrial strength?

Dates to remember

1760–1820	George III
1789	Outbreak of the French Revolution
1793	France declared war on England
1799, 1800	Combination laws passed
1805	Battle of Trafalgar
1815	Battle of Waterloo

Things to do

1 Find out the name of the prison built in England to house the French prisoners of war. What interesting hobby had they there?
2 The style of dress both for men and for women changed a great deal during these years. Make drawings of the costume of the time. A popular hair style came from Paris called 'à la Guillotine'. What was it, and why was it so called?
3 Find out the number of guns and the complement of men in the following ships of the Royal Navy: battleship, frigate, cutter, schooner, sloop.

There are many interesting people to read about at this time: Joseph Priestley, Tom Paine, Shelley, William Godwin. Novels have been written about the French Revolution; the most famous is *The Tale of Two Cities*, by Charles Dickens. Thackeray, in *Vanity Fair*, has given a wonderful description of the march of the British forces to Brussels in 1815, and the doings of the people during the Battle of Waterloo.

Things to discuss

Machinery threw men out of work at the beginning of the nineteenth century. Do you think that automation will have the same effect in the present century?

Books to read

Charles Dickens, *A Tale of Two Cities*, Nelson
M. D. Hay, *Landsman Hay*, Hart-Davis
G. Morey, *Life of Wellington*, Muller
Geoffrey Trease, *Thunder of Valmy*, Macmillan

This French print of 1803 shows various ideas for the proposed invasion of England (including an early plan for a Channel tunnel).

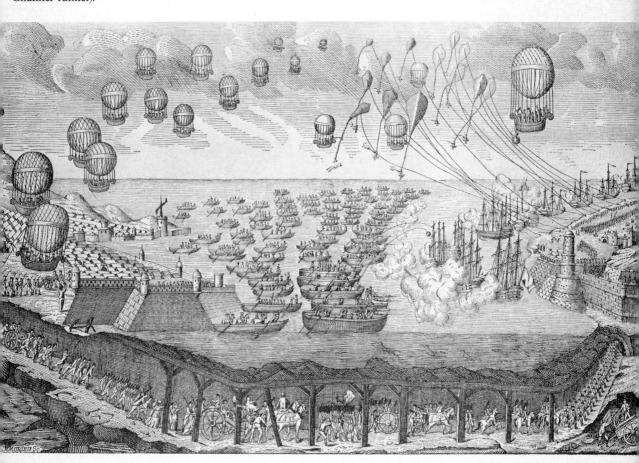

Chapter 2
After the wars

The Congress of Vienna   1815

In the high summer of 1815 Vienna was the gayest capital in Europe. Flags and banners were flying from the buildings. The streets were thronged with Kings, Princes, Grand Dukes and ambassadors, all ready to make the terms of peace. Each evening there were dinner-parties and balls. The opera house was a dazzling sight, with diamonds sparkling on the dresses of the women, and Orders on the magnificent uniforms of the men. Napoleon was said to have taken a sponge and wiped it across the map of Europe. He had overturned thrones and set up new states. The rulers who had been despoiled of their kingdoms, many of whom had lived in exile, now came back to claim their lands.

One of the most popular figures was the tall, handsome Alexander I of Russia. Austrian interests were looked after by Metternich, the Chancellor. He was a clever diplomat, who knew what he wanted and how to get it. The King of Prussia was there, a little overawed by the contrast between the splendour of the Imperial court and his own humble palace in Berlin. England sent the Foreign Secretary, Castlereagh.

Naturally, the countries which had borne the brunt of the fighting against Napoleon expected to be rewarded. Russia had her claims to the Grand Duchy of Warsaw and to Finland confirmed. Prussia was given a large slice of territory in the Rhineland. Austria gave up her possessions in the Netherlands, and took in exchange two provinces in Italy, Lombardy and Venetia. Great Britain wanted nothing in Europe. Our interests were overseas. During the war we had taken Cape Colony from the Dutch, to prevent its falling into French hands. We kept that, making a payment for it to the Dutch, and it became an English colony. We gained also a few of the West Indian islands. France was treated leniently. She paid an indemnity, but kept her territory almost intact.

The Holy Alliance

To the kings and princes in Europe the French Revolution and the wars that followed it seemed like a nightmare, which must be buried and forgotten. The makers of the treaty in Vienna believed that rulers should be absolute: that means that they should govern how they liked without consulting the wishes of their subjects. But would people in 1815 be satisfied with this kind of rule? The French had shown how an inefficient government could be removed by determined men, when they stormed the Bastille in 1789.

The Tsar Alexander proposed that the great powers should form a

Europe in 1815.

'Holy Alliance' and that the European sovereigns should live together in the spirit of Christian brotherhood. Metternich and Castlereagh were rather amused at the idea of the jealous sovereigns living like brothers. Nevertheless, the alliance was formed by Russia, Prussia and Austria; each member promised to come to the help of any ruler who was faced with rebellion in his country. France also joined, but Castlereagh refused to commit Britain. He was in favour of some sort of international cooperation. For instance he tried unsuccessfully to persuade the powers to abolish the slave trade. He was also in sympathy with the aims of the alliance, but he thought it would involve Britain in European quarrels. Britain therefore stood aloof from the Holy Alliance.

It was an uneasy peace. All the nations did not welcome their old sovereigns back. In Italy, for example, there was a strong movement in favour of democratic government, that is, government by parliament. The most extreme example of an old-fashioned sovereign was the King of Piedmont, who ordered that the years 1789 to 1815 should be removed from the calendar and no one was to mention anything which had happened during that time.

In 1820 there were revolts in Naples and Piedmont, both of them put down by the Austrian army. Later a liberal movement in Spain was defeated by French troops on the orders of Metternich. Britain took no part in these wars.

Canning

On the death of Castlereagh in 1822, Canning became Foreign Secretary. He had a more positive policy than Castlereagh had had. He was not content with simple non-interference; he prevented the Holy Alliance from interfering. When Portugal was threatened by Metternich, because he did not approve of its government, Canning sent some ships of war to Portugal to prevent any Austrian troops being landed there.

Spain had colonies in South America. They began to fight for their independence, just as the North American colonies had fought against us in 1775. Spain asked the Holy Alliance to send military help. Canning declared that the British navy would prevent any force going to the help of Spain.

This policy was warmly supported by the people in Britain. Many volunteers went to the help of the Spanish colonies, the most famous of them being Admiral Cochrane, a daring sea-dog. For many years the flagship of the Chilean navy was named *El Almirante Cochrane*. Canning made the name of Britain respected among the European liberals.

An unpopular government

> I met murder on the way –
> He had a mask like Castlereagh –
> Very smooth he looked, and grim;
> Seven bloodhounds followed him.
>
> Clothed with the Bible, as with light
> And the shadows of the night,
> Like Sidmouth, next, hypocrisy
> On a crocodile rode by.
>
> Shelley

Why did Shelley make such a bitter attack on these two men? They were prominent members of a most unpopular government, that of Lord Liverpool, which was in power after 1815. We have seen how Castlereagh did useful work at the Congress of Vienna, how he prevented Britain from lining up with the reactionary powers, and how he tried to get the slave trade abolished. Yet in England he was so much hated that men threw stones at his coffin when it was driven through the streets of London, and a man on the scaffold cried out 'Forgive them all except Castlereagh.'

To understand the hatred aroused against this government we must first look at the conditions in the country at that time. The cheering and excitement which had accompanied the end of the war were over and peace did not bring what people expected – prosperity. The war was finished, peace had come and brought with it severe unemployment.

Peace without plenty

As long as the country was at war, there were orders for munitions

Sidmouth's spies

The government specially feared unrest and disorder in the Midlands and the North, where the unemployment was greatest, so Lord Sidmouth, the Home Secretary, sent there a spy called Oliver to report about the activities in those regions. Of course a spy is better rewarded if he finds something sensational to report and Oliver determined to find some worthwhile information. He first went to Nottingham and, pretending to be a reformer, he told the people that the Londoners were disappointed that there had been no armed rising; he urged them to wait no longer but to supply themselves with arms. Some unfortunate men fell into the trap, bought arms, and were of course arrested, and two of the leaders were hanged. Oliver then went to Manchester where he knew there was a plan to march to London to see the Prince Regent and ask his help; each man would take a blanket with him and so they were known as the 'Blanketeers'. Oliver encouraged the idea of the march, hoping that some violence would break out. Fortunately the magistrates stopped the march before it had gone very far and Oliver was cheated of his ambition to get the leaders rounded up in London. He next went to Yorkshire where he told the same story and particularly tried to get a bookseller named Willans to concoct some plan for a riot. The bookseller was cautious. He noticed that, whereas Oliver's associates got arrested, he himself remained free. Then one evening he noticed that when Oliver came out of a tavern a man in livery touched his hat

In this number, Cobbett exposed a politician who had used a forged letter to slander his opponent. After reading the first edition, the politician sued Cobbett for libel, while his agent sent Cobbett a note warning him against publishing another sheet 'at his peril'. But Cobbett was not to be intimidated.

THE SUPPRESSED NUMBER.

Vol. 34, No. 24.---Price Two Pence.

COBBETT's WEEKLY POLITICAL REGISTER.

731] LONDON, SATURDAY, MARCH 6, 1819. [732

SECOND EDITION.

As notified in the Register of last week, the Publisher had been threatened with a Prosecution on account of alledged libellous matter contained in this number. The Publisher has since obtained *Proof* that he was, in publishing this Number, publishing nothing but Truth, and, therefore, unhesitatingly, prints a Second Edition.

On account of the extra trouble that has been given to Newsmen and Venders by the Suspension of the publication of this Number, the present Edition will be supplied to the Trade at Five Pounds a Thousand, or Ten Shillings a Hundred.

TO
MAJOR CARTWRIGHT.
LETTER XI.

On the Rump Farce at the Crown

ing me an Observer, an account of the farce, exhibited by the Rump, at the Crown and Anchor, on the 17th of November last. This farce, after the Rump had done all the mischief in their power; after having made a bad use of all the means which real public-spirit had put into their hands; after having, for years, intrigued for the dirtiest of purposes under the most fair professions: after having kept you out of parliament and put in an enemy of our cause; after all this, and, drawing, as they manifestly do, fast towards the close of their scandalous career, the 'present

to him and drove him away in a carriage. Mr Willans sent a letter to the *Leeds Mercury* warning men against Oliver and this saved people there from the fate of the men in Nottingham.

Peterloo   1819

The policy of repressing any meetings and arresting those who complained too loudly did not succeed. In fact many people grew disgusted with some of the actions of the government. In 1819 a meeting was planned to take place in St Peter's Fields, Manchester, to be addressed by a man nicknamed 'Orator Hunt'. People came from all parts of the town; whole families turned out, prepared for a peaceful meeting. They did not know that in all the side-streets the Yeomanry and cavalry had been placed ready to rush the crowd at the word of command. Orator Hunt had only just mounted the platform when the order was given to charge the crowd. Terrified women were pushed and tumbled in their effort to get their children away. Altogether thirteen were killed

A bitter cartoon of 'Peterloo': well-nourished soldiers are showing their courage by trampling the poor underfoot.

and hundreds wounded. One man on the platform, a printer called Carlyle, determined to get back to London to publish the account of what he saw. He managed to dive beneath the horses and catch the night coach to London and printed the full story. Indignation ran high and this meeting was called in derision 'Peterloo', remembering Waterloo when the British army had defeated the French. Castlereagh and Sidmouth made themselves still more unpopular when they publicly thanked the cavalry for their prompt action. They also passed six acts – called the 'Gagging Acts' – to make it difficult to organize meetings.

Of course, not all the members of the governing class took this harsh attitude towards the unemployed working-class. Lord Byron spoke passionately in the House of Lords against a bill to make the penalties for frame-breaking more severe. 'Is there not blood enough upon your penal code, that more must be poured out to ascend to Heaven and to testify against you? . . . Can you commit a whole country to their prisons? Will you erect a gibbet in every field and hang men like scarecrows? . . . Are these the remedies for a starving and desperate populace?' But he was in the minority.

Conditions improve after 1820

The situation began to improve when trade revived. After 1820 the nations in Europe were recovering from the war and once more orders began to come to the English mills. After the death of Castlereagh in 1822, Sidmouth resigned and new men with a more intelligent understanding of what was needed entered the Cabinet. Huskisson was at the Board of Trade and Robinson Chancellor of the Exchequer. They worked together to improve trade. Duties had been put on so many articles that it was said the only trade they encouraged was that of smuggling. Many of these duties were taken off or much reduced. Trade agreements were made with other nations and this increased the flow of trade into Britain. Huskisson also made the price of corn stable. He would have liked to reduce the price of corn further, but could not get Parliament to agree to that. However, he kept the price steady.

Trade unions

Other reforms soon followed. After a long campaign the combination laws were abolished in two acts passed in 1824 and 1825. A London tailor called Francis Place had worked hard for this. This remarkable man worked at tailoring by night, to earn his living, and by day he carried on political activity. He had an informal reading-room attached to his shop, and willingly lent books to anyone who wanted to educate himself. Of course he was not in Parliament, but he had a few radical friends there and he coached them in what they should say. One of the arguments used was that the workers only wanted to join unions because they were forbidden and, if they were legal, no one would try to form one. Trade unions which had worked in secret could now come into the open.

Penal code

Peel, who became Home Secretary, made a careful study of the criminal laws. In those days, men could be hanged for stealing something worth 6s. From this came the saying 'one might as well be hanged for a sheep as a lamb' – in other words if you risked being hanged for a small thing, you might as well steal something big. As there was always a chance that the theft would not be discovered or, because the penalties were so severe, the jury might acquit, so there were plenty of people willing to risk the consequences. Peel argued that if you wanted to deter people from crime, a certain punishment is more effective than a savage one which may not be carried out. He abolished the death penalty for more than a hundred offences. Alarmists cried out that now everyone would be robbed and murdered. Peel's code would seem brutal to us to-day, for there were still many people hanged every year, but it was merciful compared to the old code. Peel also founded the famous police force in London, and soon other towns adopted this idea. The object was to prevent crime taking place. Before that the guardians of the law in London were the Bow Street Runners, who generally ran away if there was any violence around. The police then wore top hats, dark blue coats and white trousers. They carried wooden truncheons and were not allowed to have firearms. They were nicknamed 'Peelers' and later 'Bobbies', after Sir Robert Peel. The idea was not popular at first; people said it was an infringement of the rights of Englishmen. As a result of these various reforms, and because trade was beginning to revive, the country was more prosperous than it had been in the first seven years after Waterloo.

A 'Peeler'.

The reform of Parliament   1832

In spite of these reforms, the government had plenty of critics. Not only the unemployed working-class, but also the rich manufacturers wanted a change in the form of government. Parliament, which passed our laws, was supposed to represent the people. In actual fact it represented very few of them. There were two houses, the House of Lords and the House of Commons. In the first of these sat all the peers of the realm, great landowners all of them, and twenty-four bishops. For the House of Commons, the members were elected by the counties and by the boroughs. Those boroughs which had existed in the time of Edward I, who called a Parliament in 1295, could send two members to the House of Commons. Now over the centuries some of those towns had disappeared, or for one reason or another they no longer had any importance. Such towns were called 'rotten boroughs'. Dunwich had fallen into the sea, others had just decayed away. In one there was only one man living, who boasted that at every election he sent two members to Parliament to represent him. Also, the system of voting was different in every town. In some places men who lived in certain houses could vote, in others the members were chosen by the Mayor. There was plenty of bribery, and those who were most satisfied with the system were those

Old Sarum. The mound in the centre returned two members to the House of Commons.

few voters who expected a handsome bribe at an election, and regarded that as a legitimate part of their income.

The manufacturers were left out of this. Their towns, Leeds, Bradford, Manchester, Birmingham, and all the other new industrial cities had no members because they had not existed as towns in 1295. As you would expect, the laws passed favoured the landowning interest; for example the corn laws, which were put on to please the landowners. The businessmen wanted a share in making the laws as they had their own interests to protect. They took up the cry of reform of Parliament, and the party which sponsored this idea was the Whig Party. There were others who were interested in change, the radicals. This word comes from the Latin word meaning a root; they said they went to the root of the matter, and in the case of reform they wanted to go much further than the businessmen – they wanted the vote for every man, whatever his occupation.

Cobbett was a radical, and he wrote:

It will be asked, will a reform of Parliament give the labouring man a cow or a pig; will it put bread and cheese into his satchel instead of infernal cold potatoes; will it give him a bottle of beer to carry to the field instead of making him lie down on his belly to drink out of the brook; will it put upon his back a Sunday coat and send him to Church instead of leaving him to stand lounging about shivering with an unshaven face and a carcase half covered with a ragged smock frock, with a filthy ragged shirt beneath it as yellow as a kite's

Mr Gripes and Mr Milksop are fighting an election – almost literally. Among the objects hurled in abuse is a cat. (Mr Gripes wishes to repeal a tax on beer, and his voters are already drunk.)

foot? Will Parliamentary Reform put an end to the harnessing of men and women by a hired overseer to draw carts like beasts of burden; will it put an end to the system which causes the honest labourer to be worse fed than the felons in the jails? . . . The enemies of reform jeeringly ask us, whether reform would do these things for us; and I answer distinctly THAT IT WOULD DO THEM ALL.

You can imagine how words like this would fire the enthusiasm of the people.

When a class of people has a great deal of power, it is hard to defeat them. The landlords enjoyed their position and had no intention of giving up their privilege of virtually controlling Parliament. The Whig leaders knew that only tremendous pressure from the country would make any reform possible. On the death of George IV in 1830 there was an election, and the hopes of the reformers were dashed when the Prime Minister, the Tory Duke of Wellington, declared that the British Constitution was the best that any country could have; he did not want any change at all. The result was that he was defeated on a vote in the House of Commons.

The Whigs introduce a Reform Bill

William IV then asked the Whig leader, Lord Grey, to become Prime Minister. He prepared a Reform Bill and presented it to Parliament. It

Nottingham Castle burning during the Reform Bill riots.

was thrown out because it was said to be too radical, although really it was not a very revolutionary bill. There followed another election in 1831, quite the most exciting one in our history. The people knew that the issue before the country was a clear one: Parliamentary reform or else the continued rule of the landowners.

'We want the Bill'

The whole country was seething with excitement; men marched through the streets shouting 'We want the bill, the whole bill, and nothing but the bill.' When it came to voting there were many broken heads and fights round the polling booths. The result was a victory for the Whigs, who came back with a majority. Another Reform Bill was then introduced into the House of Commons by Lord John Russell. It was a better bill than most people had expected, for it did away entirely with the old rotten boroughs and gave seats to the new towns. The struggle was not over, because a bill had to be passed by both the House of Commons and the House of Lords. The Commons passed it, but the Lords rejected it. This rejection was followed by riots all over the country. In Bristol there were four days of rioting and burning of public buildings. In Nottingham the castle was burnt. Lord Grey resigned. He said he could not carry on if the Lords opposed the measure. William IV sent for Wellington and asked him to form a ministry. For ten days there was tense excitement. Would Wellington try to rule by military force? It was obvious that the mass of the people were determined to have the bill.

In Birmingham, Mr Attwood, a progressive-minded banker, who believed that banks should serve the needs of the people, had formed a union of the lower and middle classes, suggested hitting where it hurt most. He proposed first that all members of the union should refuse to pay taxes, and secondly that all those who had funds in the Bank of England should draw them out. Finally the Birmingham Political Union prepared to march to London, 200,000 strong, and camp there on Hampstead Heath until the bill was passed.

Disturbing rumours reached the Duke of Wellington. The Scots Greys, stationed in Birmingham, were said to be fraternizing with the members of the Political Union. It was feared that if they were ordered to fire on the marchers, they might refuse to do so. The march, however, proved not to be necessary and did not take place.

After days of tense excitement, it was announced from St James's Palace that the Lords had agreed to drop their opposition to the bill. Lord Grey had persuaded King William IV to agree to create enough Whig peers to outvote the Tories in the House of Lords. Naturally the Lords did not like the idea of being swamped by a hundred or so new peers. The Duke of Wellington showed his common sense by advising the Tory Party not to oppose the bill. The country had shown clearly that it would have the Reform Bill, and that if it were not passed there might be dangerous riots. It was finally passed by the House of Lords on 4 June, 1832.

What the Reform Bill did

When we look at the terms of the bill it is surprising to find it such a mild one, hardly enough you would think to arouse so much passion. The House of Lords remained the same. The system of representation in the House of Commons was changed; the rotten boroughs were abolished, and members taken away from towns with less than 2,000 inhabitants. The new towns could elect members and more members were given to the large counties. Perhaps the most important alteration was that voting was made uniform throughout the country; in the towns, everyone who paid £10 a year in rent could vote. So the bill did away with all the antiquated systems of electing members.

£10 a year rent sounds very little, but rents then were much lower than they are now. The new voters were the merchants and business-men, the doctors, lawyers, shopkeepers. The workers – who had fought hard to get the bill passed – gained nothing. Hardly any of them qualified to vote. In the first glow of enthusiasm the defects of the bill were not noticed. The exclusive power of the landowning Tories had been broken; and once a change had been made, it would be easier in the future to widen the franchise, that is to give the right to vote to a larger number of people.

Dates to remember

1820–30	George IV
1819	Peterloo massacre
1824	Penal code reformed
1824, 1825	Combination laws repealed
1829	Police force founded
1830	Death of George IV
	Whig government in office
1832	First Reform Bill passed

Things to do

1 Go to your local library and look up a history of your town. Find out how many men had the right to vote before 1832.
2 Find out whom they returned to Parliament *before* 1832 and *after* the bill was passed.
3 How is a modern election different from one 150 years ago?
4 Find out when your town first had policemen and how many of them there were.

Charles Dickens, in *Pickwick Papers*, describes the election at Eatanswill. In the novel *Middlemarch*, by George Eliot, you can get a good idea of how people thought of the prospect of Parliamentary reform. Middlemarch is really Coventry where George Eliot lived for some years.

Interesting people to read about: William Cobbett, Robert Owen, and Elizabeth Fry, who did so much to improve prison conditions.

Books to read

A. M. D. Hughes (ed), *Cobbett: Selections*, Oxford University Press
M. St. J. Fancourt, *The People's Earl*, Longmans
G. Pattison, *Outline of Trade Union History*, Barrie & Rockliffe
N. Wymer, *Social Reformers*, Oxford University Press

Chapter 3
After the Reform Bill   1832-34

The excitement was over. Everyone thought that after the passing of the Reform Bill life would be easier and better. Actually a great number of the people who had been enthusiastic for reform had not had a clear idea of what it would mean and what they would all gain. Sydney Smith said that 'schoolboys thought there would be more plums in the pudding and old maids thought they would find husbands.'

What changes did it really make? Over 200,000 more men had the right to vote, though five out of every six in the country still had no vote. The important difference was that in the House of Commons there were members who were first of all interested in trade and manufacture, whereas before the House of Commons had been an assembly of landowners. These new men had fresh ideas. They wanted to change with the times and were willing to pass measures to bring the country up to date. There were also about a dozen radicals, among them William Cobbett, who urged the Whigs forward to make social reforms. This new Parliament, the first to be elected after the passing of the Reform Bill, was full of confidence and began well by abolishing slavery in the British Empire and by protecting the factory children.

The abolition of slavery   1833

If you were to sail now along the west coast of Africa, you might see one or two large white buildings glittering in the sun, looking like palaces. They are the old slave castles where the cargo nicknamed 'black ivory' was kept. The slave-traders bought men and women and housed them there until they could be put on ships to be carried across the Atlantic. To us now, the idea of trading in human beings and selling them into slavery seems a horrible one. In the seventeenth and eighteenth centuries it was accepted as a trade, just like any other trade. When the Spanish and the English began to colonize in America they could have as much land as they wanted, but the land was no use to them unless they had people to work it for them. They found the native Red Indians were not strong enough, so they brought over Negroes from the west coast of Africa. Ordinary kindly people invested in this business and thought there was nothing wrong in it. The slavers, as the ships were called, set out from Liverpool or Bristol, taking with them cheap metal and woollen goods which they sold to the chieftains in return for slaves. Sometimes, when they could not buy them in this way, they made raids into villages and carried off the captives.

The worst horror was perhaps the 'middle passage', as the voyage to America was called. The slaves were packed as tightly as possible

A slave hoeing on a West Indian plantation. He wears a heavy weight on his arm, and spiked anklets to prevent escape. The mask was used to prevent him eating while he worked.

SLAVES AT SALE,
WITHOUT RESERVE.
BY BEARD, CALHOUN & CO.

J. A. BEARD, Auctioneer.

WILL BE SOLD AT AUCTION ON

Tuesday, Jan. 16th,

AT 12 O'CLOCK, AT BANKS' ARCADE, THE FOLLOWING DESCRIBED NEGROES:

1. ROSIN, 13 years of age a griffe, good house boy, fine temper, fully guarantied, and speaks German and English.

2. JORDAN, 23 years of age, a likely negro, house servant and trusty waiter fully guarantied.

3. JANE, aged 24 years, a very superior washer, ironer, good American cook and house woman fully guarantied.

4. MARY, aged 24 years and child 1 year old, a trusty woman, good washer, ironer and American cook fully guarantied.

5. EDWIN, aged 27 years, a griffe man, an excellent waiter, steward, and trusty servant fully guarantied.

6. ESTHER, aged 40 years, a smart intelligent and cleanly cook, washer and ironer title only guarantied.

7. ANNE, aged 24 years, an excellent house servant, washer, ironer, and good cook, with her three children, one aged 5, another 2 and the last 1 year; they are fully guarantied, but will be sold to go into the country, by her owners instructions.

8. SAM, aged 28 years, a field hand; title only guarantied.

9. AGNES, aged 24 years, a good cook, washer and ironer fully guarantied.

10. HENRY, aged about 26 years, a field hand, and a stout man, sold as having run away from the plantation.

11. JOHN, aged 15 years, a smart waiting boy fully guarantied.

12. JANE, aged 17 years, a fine house girl and field hand fully guarantied.

13. MARY, aged 35 years, a superior nurse and house woman fully guarantied.

ALSO:

14. PATRICK, aged 28 years, a likely man, good barber, body and house servant. Sold under a good character, and fully guarantied against the vices and maladies prescribed by law.

TERMS CASH. Acts of sale before **J. R. BEARD,** Notary Public at the expense of the purchasers.

ALSO,

The following described Slaves sold for account of Mr. Henry Deacon, who failed to comply with the terms of sale made for the account of the Succession of C. H. L. ELWYN, deceased, to wit:

The Negress **MATHILDA,** aged about 29 years and her son **PAUL,** 7 years—a good washer, ironer and Cook.

TERMS CASH. Act of Sale before **H. B. CENAS,** Notary Public, at the expense of the Purchasers.

Beg's Power Press, 56 Magazine St.

Poster advertising a slave auction.

because, as the traders argued, even if many of them did die, it was worth the risk, for the profit they would make for each one they landed was enormous. This is a description of one of the slavers:

She had taken in 336 males and 226 females on the coast of Africa, making in all 562 and had been out seventeen days during which she had thrown overboard 55. The slaves were all enclosed under grated hatchways between decks. The space was so low that they sat between each other's legs, and stowed so close together that there was no possibility of their

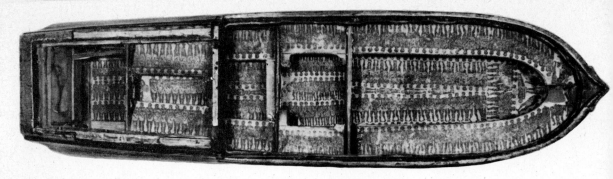

lying down, or at all changing their positions night or day. Over the hatchway stood a ferocious-looking fellow with a scourge of many twisted thongs in his hand, who was the slave-driver of the ship and whenever he heard the slightest sound below, he shook it over them and seemed eager to exercise it. But the circumstance which struck us most forcibly was, how it was possible for such a number of human beings to exist, packed up and wedged together as tight as they could cram, in low cells, three feet high, the greater part of which, except that immediately under the grated hatchways, was shut out from light or air, and this when the thermometer exposed to the open sky was standing in the shade of our decks at 89 degrees.

All through the eighteenth century every year thousands of Negroes from West Africa were taken in British ships to North and South America and to the West Indies in conditions like this.

We can learn a good deal about this trade from the journal kept by

Model of a slave ship showing how closely packed the slaves were. The model (and the poster on page 43) are from Wilberforce House, Hull, where Wilberforce was born. The house is now a museum.

WEST INDIES

tobacco cotton sugar rum

brandy wine cloth iron

slaves

WEST AFRICA

The slave triangle: European ships took goods from Europe to Africa; then took African slaves to America; and finally sailed back, carrying goods produced by slave labour in America to Europe.

one John Newton, who plied the coast of Africa for nine years, transporting slaves to the West Indies. He was a pious man, who always held services on Sunday for the crew and his diary makes frequent references to his Christian duty. Such phrases strike an odd note when we read entries like these:

Monday 11 December. By the favour of Divine Providence made a timely discovery today that the slaves were forming a plot for insurrection. Surprised two of them trying to get off their irons, and upon further search in their rooms, upon the information of three boys, found some knives, stones, shot, etc., and a cold chisel. Upon inquiry there appeared eight principally concerned to move in projecting the mischief and four boys in supplying them with the above instruments. Put the boys in irons and slightly in thumbscrews to urge them to a full confession.
Tuesday 12 December. In the morning examined the men slaves and punished six of the principal, put four of them in collars.
Friday 23 February. The boy slaves impeached the men of an intention to rise upon us. Found four principally concerned, punished them with the thumbscrews and afterwards put them in neck yokes.

Slave irons.

John Newton expressed his gratitude to God for the profit he made on these voyages. He retired for reasons of health and later became a clergyman and was a great friend of the poet Cowper. When he thought of his experiences in the slave trade he began to realize all its horror and became one of the campaigners against it. As he himself knew it at first hand, his evidence was valuable. He wrote a pamphlet on the subject and described how it degraded the seamen who worked the ships and then turned to the treatment of the slaves:

I have seen them sentenced to unmerciful whippings, continued until the poor creatures have not had the power to groan under their misery, and hardly a sign of life remained. I have seen them agonizing for hours, I believe for days together under the torture of the thumbscrews; a dreadful engine which, if the screw be turned by an unrelenting hand, can give intolerable anguish.

Wilberforce and Clarkson

One of the first people to raise his voice against slavery was Dr Johnson, who once at Oxford gave the toast 'Here's to the next insurrection of the Negroes in the West Indies.' The Quakers took up the cause of the abolition of slavery. They could not sit in Parliament because only members of the Church of England were allowed to be members, so they had to find someone who could carry on their mission in the House of Commons. They asked William Wilberforce to undertake the work; they could not have found a better champion of the slaves. For one thing he was a fine speaker; he was called 'silver tongue'. Then, too, he had influential friends who would support him in Parliament. He knew that the majority of people were ignorant of what really went on. They had no idea of all the horrors of the trade. So Wilberforce

collected his facts carefully. In this he was helped by his friend Clarkson, who interviewed sailors who worked on the slavers and got exact information. This was often difficult to get because the sailors feared they would not be employed if it was known they were giving away inconvenient facts. Whitbread, the brewer, came to the rescue. He offered to compensate anyone who lost his job through telling Clarkson what he had witnessed.

Armed with accurate information Wilberforce spoke at meetings all over the country. He wanted people to know what went on. He brought models of slave ships, showing how the unfortunates were crowded. He also showed articles he had bought in the Liverpool shops: thumbscrews, handcuffs, leg irons, and an instrument designed to force open the mouth. Some of the captives in their misery refused to eat and so had to be forcibly fed. All this brought home to people the inhumanity of the trade. In 1807, when for a few months the Whigs

Clarkson's last appearance on a public platform in June 1840, when he addressed the Anti-Slavery Convention at the Freemasons' Hall. Some women were there: they were beginning to play a part in public life.

were in power, a bill was passed making the slave trade illegal. Unfortunately it went on for many years illegally, although the British navy patrolled the west coast of Africa to intercept slavers. As far as can be reckoned the number of slaves rescued by the navy was about 150,000. Great Britain had taken a prominent part in the slave trade. It is pleasant to think that it was the British navy which was foremost in stopping the illegal trade.

Wilberforce and his friends had won the first round in the battle. How about the slaves working in the British West Indies? The chief product there was sugar and the planters had many friends in the House of Commons whose interests were bound up with the sugar industry. They fiercely resisted any suggestion of freeing the slaves. They argued that slaves would only work if they were forced to do so; if they were free, the sugar would not be produced and the British would either have to do without sugar or else pay a tremendous price for it. Also they said that the Negroes brought from Africa learned the benefits of civilization and Christianity. Those who favoured slavery painted a happy picture of life on a plantation, but the missionaries who came back described the life in very different terms.

John Newton again has evidence here. He reported a conversation he had with a planter from the island of Antigua. He said that calculations had been made with all possible exactness, to determine which was the preferable, that is the more profitable, method of managing slaves:

William Wilberforce.

Whether to appoint them moderate work, plenty of provision and such treatment as might enable them to protract their lives to old age or, by rigorously straining their strength to the utmost, with little relaxation, hard fare, and hard usage, to wear them out before they become useless, and unable to do service; and then to buy new ones to fill up their places?

He added that the skilful calculators had determined in favour of the latter mode, as much the cheaper, and he could mention several estates on the island of Antigua, on which it was known that a slave seldom lived more than nine years.

The movement to abolish slavery had support from both sides in Parliament. In 1833 an act was passed by the Whig government to end slavery in the British Empire. The day fixed was 31 July 1834, and from that time onwards the slaves on the plantations were free. Wilberforce was a very sick man when the measure was being debated, but he learnt before he died that the cause for which he had fought so hard had triumphed.

Besides the West Indies, one other part of the Empire was affected by the act against slavery; this was Cape Colony in South Africa. The Dutch farmers who lived there, who were called the Boers, resented losing their free labour. They also said the compensation paid to them by the British government was too small. In 1836 some of them trekked over the River Vaal to found their own state of Transvaal, where they were out of reach of the British government.

The Factory Act   1833

Question   What time did you begin work in a factory?
Answer   When I was six years old.
Question   What were your hours of labour at the mill?
Answer   From five in the morning until nine when they were thronged.
Question   For how long a time have you worked that excessive length of time?
Answer   For about half a year.
Question   You are considerably deformed in your person in consequence of that labour?
Answer   Yes, I am.

Inside an early factory. The machines are spinning cotton, and the young boy with the brush is employed in the dangerous task of sweeping up waste from under the machine.

   We should not expect now to have much trouble in convincing people that to work small children for sixteen hours a day would ruin their health. We have to remember that children of the poorer classes had always been expected to work; they used to pick wool from the bushes on the common, or help a little on the farm, but they worked out of doors and at their own pace. Until machinery was invented there was not much work they could do; spinning and weaving were skilled crafts. In a factory children could mind machines, pick up waste, and do other unskilled jobs. They were cheap; the average wage for a child was 3s. a week. There were some farsighted employers who condemned the long hours which children worked. When young Robert Owen went to

New Lanark to manage a cotton-spinning mill which was owned by his father-in-law, he found there 500 pauper apprentices. His father-in-law had the reputation of being a good employer. He fed the children well, employed a doctor to look after their health and insisted that they had some education. But as the hours were thirteen a day, and some of the children were only eight years old, neither good food, nor medical care, still less education were of much use to them. Owen reduced the hours of work and finally gave up employing pauper apprentices. These were orphaned children who were the responsibility of the Poor Law guardians. Even he thought that children might begin work at ten years old. There were other employers who wanted to abolish child labour. Sir Robert Peel, a mill-owner and a statesman, father of the famous Robert Peel, of whom you will read more later, got an act passed in 1819 forbidding the work of children in cotton mills before the age of ten. However, there was no means of enforcing this law, and for the most part it remained a dead letter.

The first champion of the children in Parliament was a man called Sadler. He, like Wilberforce, realized that the facts must be put before people. He got the government to agree to a commission to inquire into the state of children in the factories. The findings of this commission – from which the extract at the beginning of this section is taken – give us a picture of what life was like in the early nineteenth century. Sadler brought before the commission many people who themselves had worked as children, and also those who had been obliged through poverty to let their children work. Many were afraid to give evidence lest they lost their jobs, as indeed many of them did.

After the Reform Bill was passed Sadler lost his seat in Parliament, so someone else had to be found to carry on his work. Lord Shaftesbury was suggested. He was a remarkable man, for though he was born into a rich aristocratic family, and none of his relations were interested in social questions, he devoted his whole life to fighting for the 'underdog'. He had had a most unhappy childhood, neglected by his parents, and bullied at his first school, so that he said he cried when he had to go to school, and then cried when he had to go home. Perhaps it was this experience which made him so sensitive to the sufferings of others. He was asked when he first entered Parliament to be a member of a commission to inquire into the working of the lunacy laws. He found conditions unbelievably horrible. The lunatics were chained to the wall (see page 180), and on Sundays were left without any attention because the wardens went off duty then. Shaftesbury and the other members succeeded in getting conditions reformed, and while the inquiry was going on, Shaftesbury himself went to visit the lunatics and to bring them food every Sunday. He accepted the responsibility of piloting the Factory Act through Parliament, and worked with dogged persistence until the bill finally became law. For the rest of his life his name was connected with every measure for the welfare of children.

The report of Sadler's commission gave him plenty of ammunition

Lord Shaftesbury.

when he went into the attack. Here is another extract taken down from a worsted-spinner in Bradford, whose hours of work had been from five in the morning until eight at night with only one forty-minute break.

Question   Did you not become very drowsy and sleepy towards the end of the day and feel much fatigued?

Answer   Yes, that began about three o'clock and grew worse, and it became very bad towards six or seven.

Question   What means were taken to keep you at work so long?

Answer   There were three overlookers, one head overlooker, one to grease the machines, and one to strap.

Question   How far did you live from the mill?

Answer   A good mile.

Question   Was it painful for you to walk?

Answer   Yes, in the morning I could scarcely walk, and my brother and sister used out of kindness to take me under each arm, and run with me to the mill, and my legs dragged on the ground. In consequence of the pain I could not walk.

Girls hauling coal.

What arguments do you suppose people could bring to oppose the bill brought in by Shaftesbury? They sound strange to us now. In the first place it was said that to make any law limiting hours of work was to curtail the freedom and liberty of the mill-owner. Others said that children were better off in the factory than running about the streets, because they learned habits of industry. One member who was genuinely concerned for the children thought that work with bread was better than no bread. William Cobbett introduced a note of common sense into the discussion in the House of Commons when he said that

at one time he had thought that the navy was the great support of England, at another time her maritime commerce, at another her colonies, at another her bank. Now it was to be admitted that our great stay and bulwark was to be found in the labour of thirty thousand little girls, or rather one-eighth of that number. Yes, because it was asserted that if those little girls worked two hours a day less, our manufacturing superiority would depart from us.

Children picking up coal in a mine.

A Factory Act became law in July 1833. The provisions were that no child under nine was to work in a cotton, woollen or flax mill. No child under thirteen was to be employed for more than forty-eight hours a week, no one under eighteen for more than sixty-nine hours a week.

These provisions do not seem very generous to us. Silk and lace mills were not mentioned, nor coalmines. Nevertheless, it is one of the most important acts passed in the century, because for one thing it accepted the principle that Parliament could and would interfere with the way industry was run, and it was important because inspectors were appointed to see that it was carried out. In 1842 the work of women and children in coalmines was forbidden and in 1844 the Factory Act was applied to lace and silk mills. Neither of these measures had to face such fierce opposition as the first one had faced. Parliament had given up the old idea of letting things alone; it had accepted the duty of looking after those who could not look after themselves.

Boys being exercised in a prison yard. There were then no special magistrates for children and they were sent to ordinary prisons.

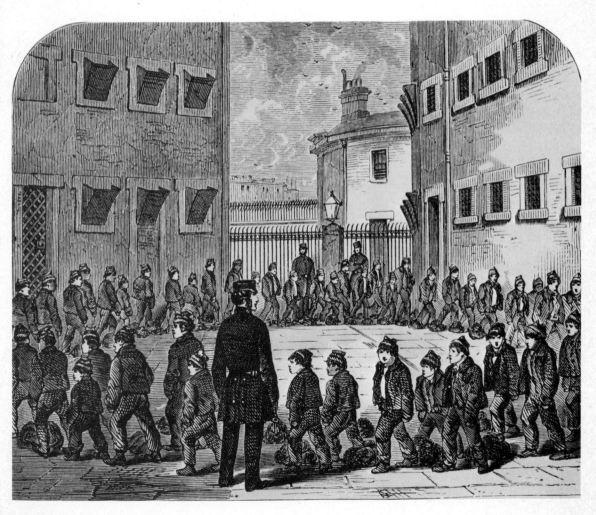

CAUTION.

WHEREAS it has been represented to us from several quarters, that mischievous and designing Persons have been for some time past, endeavouring to induce, and have induced, many Labourers in various Parishes in this County, to attend Meetings, and to enter into Illegal Societies or Unions, to which they bind themselves by unlawful oaths, administered secretly by Persons concealed, who artfully deceive the ignorant and unwary,—WE, the undersigned Justices think it our duty to give this PUBLIC NOTICE and CAUTION, that all Persons may know the danger they incur by entering into such Societies.

ANY PERSON who shall become a Member of such a Society, or take any Oath, or assent to any Test or Declaration not authorized by Law—

Any Person who shall administer, or be present at, or consenting to the administering or taking any Unlawful Oath, or who shall cause such Oath to be administered, although not actually present at the time—

Any Person who shall not reveal or discover any Illegal Oath which may have been administered, or any Illegal Act done or to be done—

Any Person who shall induce, or endeavour to persuade any other Person to become a Member of such Societies,

WILL BECOME

Guilty of Felony,

AND BE LIABLE TO BE

Transported for Seven Years.

ANY PERSON who shall be compelled to take such an Oath, unless he shall declare the same within four days, together with the whole of what he shall know touching the same, will be liable to the same Penalty.

Any Person who shall directly or indirectly maintain correspondence or intercourse with such Society, will be deemed Guilty of an Unlawful Combination and Confederacy, and on Conviction before one Justice, on the Oath of one Witness, be liable to a Penalty of TWENTY POUNDS, or to be committed to the Common Gaol or House of Correction, for THREE CALENDAR MONTHS; or if proceeded against by Indictment, may be CONVICTED OF FELONY, and be TRANSPORTED FOR SEVEN YEARS.

Any Person who shall knowingly permit any Meeting of any such Society to be held in any House, Building, or other Place, shall for the first offence be liable to the Penalty of FIVE POUNDS; and for every other offence committed after Conviction, be deemed Guilty of such Unlawful Combination and Confederacy, and on Conviction before one Justice, on the Oath of one Witness, be liable to a Penalty of TWENTY POUNDS, or to Commitment to the Common Gaol or House of Correction, FOR THREE CALENDAR MONTHS; or if proceeded against by Indictment may be

CONVICTED OF FELONY,
And Transported for SEVEN YEARS.

COUNTY OF DORSET.
Dorchester Division

February 22d. 1834.

C. B. WOLLASTON,
JAMES FRAMPTON,
WILLIAM ENGLAND,
THOS. DADE,
JNO. MORTON COLSON.

HENRY FRAMPTON,
RICHD. TUCKER STEWARD,
WILLIAM R. CHURCHILL,
AUGUSTUS FOSTER.

The Grand National Consolidated Trades Union 1834

The working-classes still had grievances. They argued that the Reform Bill had done nothing for them at all; wages had not risen and now with a slump in trade there were more unemployed. Trade Unions were now legal, many of them had been organized in the different trades, but unfortunately for the members they had not been successful in gaining wage increases by strike action. They had not enough money to hold out for long. If the unions were too small to be effective, why not have one large union and let all the workers combine? This plan was suggested by some of the leaders, and it received the warm support of Robert Owen, who said that if all trades combined they would win better conditions. A union called the Grand National Consolidated Trades Union was formed and quickly enrolled half a million members. Some people suggested that it was even larger than this. We cannot be certain of the exact figure. In any case it was sufficient to frighten the Whig government, the members of which disliked Trade Unions quite as much as the Tories had done. The manufacturers with their eyes on their profits had no wish to increase wages.

The report of the formation of this union reached a little village called Tolpuddle in Dorset, and inspired George Loveless, a Methodist preacher, to organize a Friendly Society. Wages of farm-workers in the village were 8s. a week, whilst in the neighbouring counties they were 9s. The members of the society hoped to get their wages raised if they held together and bargained with the farmers, who had earlier promised 10s. a week, but had never kept their promise. One of those who joined was gardener to a local magistrate, and he described to his master the ceremony of joining. Each man was blindfolded and with his hand on the Bible had to swear not to reveal what was said at the meeting. This was a harmless ceremony, which had been used by all the old Friendly and Benefit societies. However, word of this was sent to Melbourne, the Home Secretary, who after consulting lawyers, decided that it was illegal to take this oath.

Early one cold February morning George Loveless was roused by the constable and taken with six other villagers to be lodged in Dorchester jail. They were bewildered and confused, not having the slightest idea that they had committed any crime. They were tried and found guilty of swearing an illegal oath, contrary to an act which did indeed exist, but which was only meant to apply to the armed forces. George Loveless spoke from the dock:

My Lord, if we have violated any law, it was not done intentionally; we have injured no man's character, reputation, person or property. We were uniting together to preserve ourselves, our wives and our children from utter degradation and starvation. We challenge any man or any number of men to prove we have acted or intended to act different from that statement.

The judge sentenced them to seven years 'transportation'. Times had changed since the era of Castlereagh and Sidmouth, when men had been

Poster of February 1834, warning men against joining unions and taking illegal oaths.

transported simply for holding a meeting, and when there was no strong movement to prevent such things happening. Several members of Parliament joined the Dorchester Committee which was formed to get the men brought back. They led a deputation representing 30,000 people to the House of Commons. After two years all the men were granted a free pardon and a passage home.

The judgement did, however, have the effect of frightening the farm-workers from joining a union; it was fifty years before another one was organized. The Grand National itself only lasted about eighteen months. It was too large and unwieldy; miners from Durham could not understand the problems of Lancashire cotton-spinners, or London bricklayers. It seemed at first a wonderful idea, but turned out to be impracticable.

The New Poor Law   1834

The Poor Law certainly needed to be reformed. It dated from the days of Queen Elizabeth, when each parish had been ordered to raise a rate called the Poor Rate, the money from which was to be spent in looking after the sick and the destitute and to teach the orphan children a trade. This law had worked fairly well so long as people had stayed in one village all their lives. When men began to move round in search of work, difficulties arose because the villagers objected to supporting strangers who had come in hoping to get work. Sometimes parishes refused to let anyone settle for fear he might 'come on the rates'.

A protest against the deportation of the 'Tolpuddle Martyrs' held in April 1834. This picture gives an idea of the size of the demonstration.

Then during the Napoleonic Wars, when prices rose and there was great distress in the country, some magistrates at Speenhamland in Berkshire met to discuss the situation. They decided that when wages went below a certain amount, they must be made up out of the rates. The intention was good, but the effects were bad. It meant that farmers need not pay a decent wage, because extra money would be given from the rates to the workers who had too many children to support on their wages. Small farmers who employed no labour had to pay rates which went to make up the wages of those employed by the big farmers. Worst of all, the farm-labourer became a kind of pauper. This system was carried out in most of the southern counties of England. The government – alarmed at the rising rates – appointed a commission to inquire into the working of the Poor Law. The most important man on this commission was Chadwick, who made himself intensely unpopular by his manner of dealing with the problem.

Chadwick was conscientious and had a passion for efficiency and for economy. He inspected some of the workhouses and found the accounts were not properly kept; money was being embezzled by the workhouse masters. In some villages he found that nearly everyone was living partly 'off the rates'. Unfortunately Chadwick saw only one side of the problem. He did not understand that extreme poverty due to low wages was causing the farm-workers to become paupers, compelled to depend on the rates. He decided that all outdoor relief should be stopped. Out-

Refuge for destitute females, with a row of coffin-like beds on the right.

George Cruikshank's drawing of Oliver Twist 'asking for more'.

door relief meant the money that was paid out from the rates to a man living in his own home. If a man were starving then he must go into the workhouse, and before he went in, he must first part with all his possessions so that he might be really completely destitute. The workhouse must be made unpleasant so that as many as possible would avoid going there. Chadwick's argument was a simple one. Nobody likes doing disagreeable things. Make the workhouse disagreeable and men will not go there. There would have been common sense in this argument if the unfortunate destitute could have found work. Where could they get it during periods of wide unemployment? Chadwick also argued that the farmers would be forced to pay higher wages and so would relieve the burden on the rates. In fact wages did rise during the next twenty years, but they did not rise immediately. It is sometimes said that Chadwick's policy was a necessary surgical operation. In this case the operation lasted a long time and the patient had no anaesthetic.

Dickens has described in *Oliver Twist* what the workhouses were like. When Chadwick turned his attention from the south to the north of England he found such vigorous opposition that the New Poor Law was never actually carried out. The factory-workers had never had a regular dole, like the farm-workers in the south. They only had poor relief when occasionally a mill shut down or went on short time. They nicknamed these new workhouses 'Bastilles'. A sudden slump in trade might turn out 400 workers in a town. Were they then to sell up their

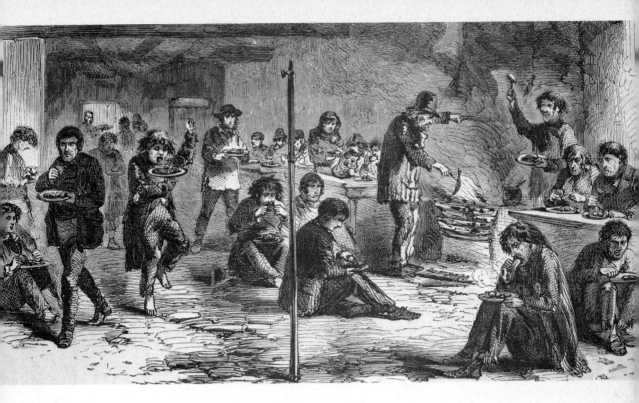

Dinner at a cheap lodging
house.

'The poor man's friend.' A
cartoon from *Punch*.

homes and go into a workhouse? It was clearly impossible to carry out such a policy and it had to be modified to allow some outdoor relief. The name of Chadwick was detested by the workers in the north.

The Whigs grow unpopular   1834

It was not long before men began to grumble about the Whigs. The middle-class people thought they were spending too much money and they objected to the taxes. It had been quite expensive to free the slaves because the government had had to spend a great deal on compensation to the owners. The Whigs were not very clever at managing the finances of the country. They had to raise more money somehow and took the easiest way out; they put taxes on goods coming into the country. This was going back on what Huskisson had done, and the effect on trade was bad. It made our own goods dearer, and consequently sales dropped off. There was a bad slump in trade and naturally the government was blamed.

How far had the Whigs justified the high hopes people had when the Reform Bill was passed? They had certainly been responsible for some useful acts. Not only had they abolished slavery and given protection to children in the mills; they had also passed an act to improve the condition of towns and had spent money on the education of children. You will read about these two last acts in later chapters. On the other hand, they had disappointed the rich middle-class by putting duties on raw materials, and they had angered the working-class by the severity of the Poor Law. Both these classes attacked them, the middle-class had one remedy and the working-class had another. We shall see in the next chapter how the Tories dealt with the situation.

Dates to remember

1830–7   William IV
1807   Abolition of slave trade
1833   Factory Act
         Abolition of slavery act
1834   Trial of the Dorchester labourers
         New Poor Law

Things to do

1   Find out from other books when slavery was abolished in
    a   the French colonies,
    b   the United States of America,
    c   Mexico.
2   What laws now exist for the protection of children?
3   Find out where your local workhouse used to be. What is it used for now?

4   Many people objected to compensating the slave-owners for the loss of their property because they said the plantation-owners never had a right to own human beings. Do you think the government was wise to give compensation?

Interesting people to read about: Wilberforce, Lord Shaftesbury, Richard Oastler.

Books to read

Charles Dickens, *Oliver Twist*, Penguin
Mrs Gaskell, *Cranford*, Nelson
J. Kamm, *They served the People*, Bodley Head
M. Marston, *Sir Edwin Chadwick*, Leonard Parsons (1925)
Rhoda Power, *We too were there*, Allen & Unwin

The royal family tree.
Queen Victoria was related, through her children, to nine European royal families.

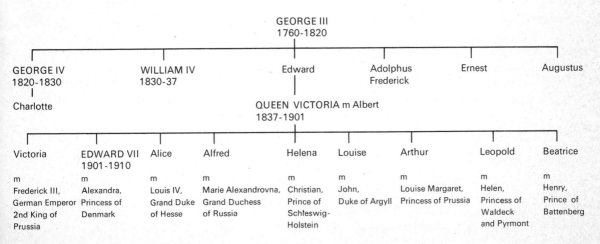

Chapter 4
England 1834

We have so far said nothing about who was reigning in England during this period. The important business of state, the making of war and the signing of peace, was carried out by the Prime Minister; the King had to sign every bill which was passed in Parliament, but in nearly all cases this had become a formality. Not many people saw the King, for he made few public appearances. They prayed for him in Church every Sunday and they saw his head on the coins of the realm. George III was reigning at the time this book begins; he had a long reign, from 1760 until 1820, and it was not a successful one. When he tried to interfere with affairs, the results were usually unhappy. For the last ten years of his reign he lived in retirement at Kew, both blind and mad. Yet people had an affection for him. He was simple and kindly and was nicknamed 'Farmer George', because of his interest in his farm at Windsor.

His eldest son, also called George, was Regent when his father was incapable of ruling. Early in life he had married a Catholic lady, Maria Fitzherbert, then denied that he had done so, and married a cousin, Caroline of Brunswick, on condition that Parliament would pay his debts. He soon deserted his wife, and their only daughter Charlotte died in 1817. When the Regent, on the death of his father, became George IV, his wife, who had been leading a dissolute life abroad, returned and expected to be crowned Queen. George gave strict orders that she was not to be admitted to Westminster Abbey. There was an unseemly scuffle at the door of the Abbey when the unfortunate woman was forced away. George hardly added to the dignity of the occasion by ogling the ladies during the ceremony. A few months later Queen Caroline died. George took no interest in the affairs of his people. The starving workers of the North, the disbanded soldiers begging in the streets, left him unmoved. He boasted of being 'the first gentleman of Europe' and was more interested in his clothes (he ordered 600 suits in one year) than in the condition of the people. It can be said in his favour that he had an interest in the arts. He admired Jane Austen so much that he always carried round with him a set of her works.

On the death of George IV in 1830 his brother William came to the throne. He was a jovial, good-natured man, a little absurd and apt to embarrass his ministers by his foolish speeches. It is understandable that the British public had very little respect for the Royal family.

Medals of George III *(above)* and George IV. What year is the medal of George IV? A family tree is on page 59.

The young Queen Victoria driving through the city of London at the beginning of her reign amid waving, cheering crowds.

Queen Victoria   1837–1901

William IV died in 1837 and was succeeded by his niece Victoria, who was just eighteen years old. Her birthday on 24 May is now kept as Commonwealth Day. She was slight, fair-haired and blue-eyed, and had a pretty complexion. The country was used to kings who were old. Now suddenly a fairy princess had burst upon the scene. Every time Victoria drove out, she was cheered by enthusiastic crowds. She herself was radiantly happy. After a strict and secluded childhood she found herself the greatest and most important sovereign in the world. Not only was she Queen of Great Britain, she also reigned over Canada and Australia and a large part of India. She possessed Buckingham Palace, St James's Palace, and Windsor Castle. She had a collection of priceless jewels and could deck herself out in diamonds every evening if she wished. Every morning, Lord Melbourne, her Prime Minister, came and explained to her all the tiresome business of government in a charming way. In the afternoon she could ride and in the evening dance. Everyone had to bow or curtsey to her. When she was crowned in Westminster Abbey not only the peers, but her elderly uncles as well, had to kiss her hand. Think what it meant to Victoria to wake in the morning and know she was Queen of England. At that time there were monarchs in every country: a Tsar in Russia, an Emperor in Austria and Kings and Princes in Germany and Italy. Most of them were old, and she, a girl of eighteen, was the most important of them all. She was full of pride in her country and was literally 'as happy as a queen'.

Victoria became devoted to Lord Melbourne and relied entirely on his judgement. She had spent her girlhood in Kensington Palace surrounded by the ladies-in-waiting of her mother and had little knowledge of the world outside the narrow court society. For the first time she came in contact with a clever, cultivated statesman who knew how to make his conversation attractive. After two years, in 1839, Melbourne told her he could no longer command a majority of supporters in the House of Commons; people wanted the Tories back. He told the Queen to summon the Tory leader, Sir Robert Peel. Victoria was dismayed. She found Peel cold and stiff. When he told her she must dismiss her ladies-in-waiting and appoint Tories, she refused, and insisted that Lord Melbourne should remain Prime Minister. This was the last time that a sovereign was able to keep a Prime Minister against the wishes of Parliament.

Alas for the fickleness of public opinion. Once hailed as a fairy princess, in 1839, after two years on the throne, she was now unpopular and was even hissed when she went to the races. The public resented her determination to retain the services of Melbourne. But however they might criticize, they were anxious for her to stay on the throne and to marry, because if she died without children, the next heir to the throne would be her uncle the Duke of Cumberland, the most unpopular of all the sons of George III. It was whispered he had killed his valet. She had known for some time that her relations had wanted her to marry her cousin, Prince Albert of Saxe-Coburg-Gotha. In the autumn of 1839 the Prince visited England and the marriage was arranged. They were married in February 1840. Victoria became very fond of her husband and gradually lost her girlish adoration of Lord Melbourne. The Prince was serious-minded and a good deal cleverer than his wife. He was able to persuade the Queen that she must not identify herself with one party only, and in 1841 she agreed without demur to Peel's becoming Prime Minister.

Victoria and Albert had nine children. They received a prim and severe education. Though Victoria lamented her own lonely childhood, she had little sympathy for her own children. Her eldest son, afterwards Edward VII, was in the charge of tutors who had to report each day on his progress to his parents. When he was occasionally allowed to invite a few boys to Windsor, his father was always present and was rather a damper on any enjoyment.

The Chartists 1838–48

Life might go on smoothly in Buckingham Palace. Outside there was plenty of agitation and political activity. When Queen Victoria came to the throne she was presented with many loyal addresses from towns and from societies. Among them was one which must have puzzled her—a letter from the London Workingmen's Association. After the usual wishes for the prosperity of the country had been expressed, there followed this statement: 'We find the bulk of the nation toiling slaves from birth to

'The Penny Black', the world's first adhesive postage stamp, issued in Great Britain on 6 May 1840.

William Lovett (*above*) and
Thomas Cooper.

death – thousands wanting food or subsisting on the barest pittance.'
Victoria had never seen the toiling slaves. How could she understand
that behind those decorated streets the destitute lived? All she saw was
smiling, cheering crowds.

The London Workingmen's Association was founded by a cabinet-
maker called William Lovett. The object of the society had been at first to
help printers who got into trouble for printing radical pamphlets. The
members met weekly and discussed politics and other matters. There
was in London a higher proportion of well-paid artisans than in any other
city, because the court was there and so there was a demand for
luxury articles such as jewellery and fine furniture. These men had more
time to study and could also afford to buy books. Lovett wanted the
working-class to have time for reading and education. He believed that
only through education would they be able to improve conditions. One
night in 1838 when several of them were meeting in Lovett's house, a
member read out six points which he considered were the first things for
which they should aim. Another member jumped up and said 'That is the
People's Charter.' The name stuck. The document was called simply the
Charter, and those who supported it were the Chartists.

The six points were:
1   Manhood suffrage, which meant that every man should have a vote;
    no one then thought of giving women the vote, so they were not
    included.
2   Secret ballot, so that no one should know how a man voted.
3   Abolition of the property qualification for members of Parliament.
4   Payment of M.P.s. These last two points would enable a poor man
    to sit in Parliament.
5   Annual Parliaments, which would have meant an election every
    year.
6   Equal electoral districts, which would mean that every con-
    stituency would have roughly the same number of voters.

You will notice that there is nothing in these points about wages
or hours of work, or prices, or houses, or the Poor Law; yet these were
the questions which were in men's minds at that time. The Chartists
believed that if all the people could vote, they would choose
members of Parliament who would carry out all the necessary
reforms. They thought the Reform Bill of 1832 had been good, but it
had not gone far enough. The reasoning was straightforward; give
the majority of people the vote, and the laws passed will be in the
interests of the majority of the people.

The campaign for the Charter

The Charter made an immediate appeal to thousands and it is easy to
see why. It was simple, there was no room for argument over something which was plain common sense. The London Workingmen's Association called a conference in Birmingham to launch the Charter in
1839, two years after Victoria had become queen. The old Birmingham

The Six Points

OF THE

PEOPLE'S

CHARTER.

1. A VOTE for every man twenty-one years of age, of sound mind, and not undergoing punishment for crime.

2. THE BALLOT.—To protect the elector in the exercise of his vote.

3. No PROPERTY QUALIFICATION for Members of Parliament —thus enabling the constituencies to return the man of their choice, be he rich or poor.

4. PAYMENT OF MEMBERS, thus enabling an honest trades-man, working man, or other person, to serve a constituency, when taken from his business to attend to the interests of the country.

5. EQUAL CONSTITUENCIES, securing the same amount of representation for the same number of electors, instead of allowing small constituencies to swamp the votes of large ones.

6. ANNUAL PARLIAMENTS, thus presenting the most effectual check to bribery and intimidation, since though a constituency might be bought once in seven years (even with the ballot), no purse could buy a constituency (under a system of universal suffrage) in each ensuing twelvemonth; and since members, when elected for a year only, would not be able to defy and betray their constituents as now.

Subjoined are the names of the gentlemen who embodied these principles into the document called the "People's Charter," at an influential meeting held at the British Coffee House, London, on the 7th of June, 1837:—

Daniel O'Connell, Esq., M.P.,	Mr. Henry Hetherington.
John Arthur Roebuck, Esq., M.P.	Mr. John Cleave.
John Temple Leader, Esq., M.P.	Mr. James Watson.
Charles Hindley, Esq., M.P.	Mr. Richard Moore.
Thomas Perronet Thompson, Esq., M.P.	Mr. William Lovett.
William Sharman Crawford, Esq., M.P.	Mr. Henry Vincent.

W. COLLINS, PRINTER, "WEEKLY TIMES" OFFICE, DUDLEY.

The People's Charter. One of the points, annual parliaments, has never been gained. What are the arguments for and against such a measure?

Political Union, which had worked so hard for the Reform Bill, was still active and its members rushed to join the new movement. The number of delegates, who came from all over the kingdom, from Scotland to Cornwall, surprised Lovett. They came for various reasons. Did a man want a decent house to live in? He joined the Chartists. Did he want his children to have a chance of some education? He joined the Chartists. Did he want to get rid of the New Poor Law? He joined the Chartists. Did he want to get the Ten Hours Bill passed? He joined the Chartists. Everything, they thought, would be possible once people could vote. Thomas Cooper, a shoemaker turned journalist, who worked in Leicester, was going home in the early hours one Sunday morning, and as he walked down a long street from every house he heard the click-click of the stocking frame. He was appalled at the thought that men had to work not only all day on Sunday but through the night to earn enough to support their families. He joined the Chartists.

How was the Charter to be made law?

Unfortunately though all the supporters agreed that they wanted the Charter to pass into law, they did not agree as to how it could be done. It was decided to get as many signatures as possible to a petition and to present it to the House of Commons. To Lovett this seemed sufficient. As he was a reasonable man, he assumed that everyone else was moved by reason, and that if Parliament were shown how widespread was the support for these six points it would agree to them. The millhands in the north were more impatient. All their pent-up fury against the New Poor Law (of which you read on page 54) was released into working for the Charter. An Irishman, O'Connor, led the northern group and edited a weekly paper called *The Northern Star*. When the government heard that some of the Chartists were drilling at night on the moors – as the Luddites had done forty years before – they sent General Napier to the north to keep order. O'Connor realized that the Chartists would be no

Troops at Euston Station. They are being sent by train to quell Chartist agitation in the north. Peelers, on foot, keep the crowd in order with fists and truncheons.

match for troops and he never supported armed rebellion. Only in one district, in South Wales, did the Chartists try by force to free some of the prisoners from the jail, and they were rounded up by soldiers and the leader, John Frost, was transported to Australia for life. The petition, when it was handed in, perhaps contained 600,000 signatures. It was rejected by Parliament with contempt. Lovett and several other leaders were arrested and given prison sentences. Undismayed, the Chartists prepared to present a larger petition, and to call a general strike if it were refused again. However, the second petition was no better received than the first and the plan of a general strike was given up.

The end of the movement

There was a final attempt in 1848, encouraged by movements abroad where popular forces were driving the rulers off their thrones. A meeting organized on Kennington Common was to be followed by a march carrying the petition to the House of Commons.

The government permitted the meeting but forbade the march. In order to ensure that there was no damage to property the Duke of Wellington was asked to be responsible for the defence of London. The people were advised to keep their windows shuttered and not to stir

Sketch of a Chartist crowd at Blackfriars Bridge on its way to the meeting at Kennington Common. It was forbidden to cross to the south bank and march to Westminster as planned.

A cartoon from *Punch* satirizing the presentation of the Charter to the House of Commons. The butler promises that his mistress will attend to this 'bill' in due course as she attends to all others – that is, by leaving them unpaid.

abroad. The meeting was peaceful and the petition as arranged was carried by the leaders to the House of Commons. The timid Londoners emerged from their houses to learn there had been neither violence nor rioting. For the third time the Charter was rejected.

Permanent results of the Chartist movement

Was the Chartist movement then a complete failure? Not one of the six points was gained, hundreds of the supporters had been transported and some of them imprisoned, and at the end of it no one was any better off. But this is not really the whole story. If you look at the end of the chapter you will see the dates on which some of the six points were finally granted. The struggle to enlarge the franchise, that is to give the vote to a wider range of people, was given an impetus by the Chartist movement, and people learned through it to organize peacefully for what they wanted. Although the movement as such disappeared, the aims of the Chartists were still fought for. They had worked against heavy odds; they had little money, and little support in Parliament, and the newspapers were against them. They left behind them a heroic legend and even in the twentieth century you can find people who boast that their grandparents or great-grandparents had been Chartists.

The Anti-Corn Law League

While the Chartists were struggling to get their petition received by Parliament, another movement, led by Bright and Cobden, was sweeping the country. Bright was a cotton manufacturer and an impassioned orator. His friend Cobden supplied him with all the necessary facts and arguments. They wanted to abolish the import duty on corn which made bread dear. Their policy was free trade, that is to say, to allow goods to go out of the country and to come into the country freely without any tax. Theirs was the policy of the manufacturers and they faced the strong opposition of the landowners in the House of Lords.

Taxes may be put on goods coming into the country for two reasons. First, they may be imposed to help home industry. If, for instance, a tax were put on woollen goods coming into England, it might help the industry at home by making the foreign goods dearer, so that fewer people bought them. The second reason is to make money for the government. If a tax is put on something which we do not produce at home, such as tea or coffee, it is a money-raising, not a protective, duty. The manufacturers in Great Britain at this time wanted free trade so that there would be cheap food and low wages, and also to enable them to buy the raw materials for their industries cheaply.

England grew corn, but not enough to feed the people. Bright and Cobden argued that if food were cheaper, men would have more money to spend on other goods, trade would therefore revive and the country grow more prosperous. They saw that keeping up the price of bread artificially was hampering trade. Peel, who was Prime Minister after 1841, understood this. He had, however, made a solemn promise that whatever else he did, he would never touch the Corn Laws. The landlords argued that the farmers and the labourers alike would be ruined if the price of corn dropped. Meanwhile the two champions of cheap food were holding monster meetings all over the country. Cheap food is always a popular cry. They made more and more recruits to their movement. Most of the Chartists held aloof from it because they suspected that it was a trick to bring down wages.

Repeal of the Corn Laws   1846

When Peel became Prime Minister in 1841 he promised that he would keep on the Corn Laws. He took duties off many goods so that on raw materials no more than five per cent duty could be levied. He knew this would stimulate trade, because it made the goods cheaper and therefore more would be sold. This would not happen at once, so to raise revenue during the period of poor trade he put on an income tax, hoping to take it off in three years' time, when trade ought to have revived. He actually never did take if off and it has gone on ever since.

The end of the Corn Laws came in a tragic way. There was a complete failure of the potato crop in Ireland, where there were villages in which nearly all the people died of hunger. The disaster was at first hardly believed; when Peel realized the desperate situation he bought maize

'The Free Trade Hat'.
Mr Marriott, a hatter, issued
free-trade propaganda inside
the crowns of the hats he sold.
He probably did better trade
because of it!

meal to send to Ireland. But the Irish ports had the same customs duties
as English ones because Ireland was governed as part of England. If the
maize and other grains were to be allowed free of duty into the Irish
ports, it would be necessary to let them also come free into English ports.

Peel was in a dilemma. He had promised to keep on these laws. But
could he let the Irish starve? He had made a promise to his party. Once
before, nearly twenty years ago, he had broken a promise when he voted
for Catholic Emancipation, granting the Catholics the same rights as
Protestants. He had been taunted then with breaking a promise. He now

had to admit again that he had changed his mind. However, it is only obstinate and stupid people whose opinions never alter; events had shown Peel that he would have to repeal the Corn Laws, and this was carried out in 1846. He was bitterly attacked for this by his own party in Parliament, and one of the attacks came from a surprising quarter; the young Disraeli, to whom Peel had been very kind, made a scornful and slashing speech, in which he compared Peel to an admiral who steers his fleet into an enemy port. But Peel had too much courage to turn aside from carrying out an unpopular act which he thought was necessary. He realized that his support for the repeal of the Corn Laws would mean that his

Punch's monument to Peel.

party would reject him. After the repeal had become law he resigned as Prime Minister and died four years later.

The repeal of the Corn Laws marked the end of the struggle between the landowners and manufacturers. From this date onwards England was governed in the interests of industry, and farming took second place.

Did repeal add to our happiness and prosperity? Many people thought so. Years later, when Bright was addressing a meeting, three very old men walked twenty miles to hear him, and wept when they saw him, because, as one of them said, 'You saved my family from starving by your work to get the Corn Laws off.'

Dates to remember

1837–1901	Queen Victoria's reign
1839	Chartist Petition launched in Birmingham
1846	Corn Laws repealed
1867	Second Reform Act. Vote given to town householders
1872	Secret Ballot Act
1884	Vote given to agricultural workers

Things to do

1 Find out who was reigning in 1837 in France, Prussia, Russia, Naples, Belgium and Piedmont.
2 Find out what foodstuffs, if any, have to pay a duty on entering this country now.

Interesting people to read about: William Lovett, Feargus O'Connor, John Bright.

Things to discuss

Many people said it would be wrong to give the vote to people who could not read. The same argument is sometimes used now when Africans demand the right to vote. Do you agree?

Books to read

A. H. Booth, *Queen Victoria*, Muller
J. Kent, *Elizabeth Fry*, Batsford
J. Laver and Brooke, *English Costume of the Nineteenth Century*, Black

Chapter 5
The royal family and foreign affairs 1848-65

For twenty years after the repeal of the Corn Laws the Tory Party was out of office, except two short periods when Lord Derby was Prime Minister. During this time the two parties changed their names; the Whigs called themselves the Liberals and the Tories took the name of Conservative. Some followers of Peel – for example Gladstone – joined the Liberals.

The Queen and Lord Palmerston

The most prominent politician during these years was the Foreign Secretary, Lord Palmerston. He was jovial, witty and immensely popular in the country. But neither the Queen nor her husband, the Prince Consort, had any trust in him. Queen Victoria realized that she was a constitutional monarch, which meant that she had to agree to what Parliament wanted and could not actively interfere in affairs at home. She thought, however, that foreign policy was different and in this sphere she claimed some rights. She was related to many of the Euro-

The centres of the revolutions, 1848.

pean sovereigns, and foreign policy seemed to her almost a family affair. Lord Palmerston was a great trial to her, for he would gaily send off important dispatches without first showing them to the Queen. When she complained he was profuse in his apologies and assured her that it would not happen again. But it did. The Queen could do nothing about it, for Palmerston was so popular that the people would have resented any interference from the throne.

The year 1848 was the 'year of revolutions', when one after another the European rulers were driven from their thrones; Victoria was horrified that anyone should dare to treat royalty in such a fashion. She knew, for instance, that the King of Naples and Sicily was an oppressive ruler, and she disapproved of him, but she disapproved still more of the people who had rebelled against him. To turn against one's sovereign was in her eyes always a sin and a crime. Palmerston, on the other hand, had an Englishman's contempt for the petty foreign princelings, and he took no pains to conceal his feeling that they had deserved what they got. The following year, 1849, most of them were restored to their thrones, and the radical leaders, when they managed to escape, came to England which was then a refuge for people who fled from their governments. Karl Marx was a refugee in London when he wrote the book *Das Kapital*, which became the foundation for the kind of socialism which was later set up in Russia. One-quarter of the people of the world now live according to the ideas worked out by Karl Marx in the famous

Cartoon by the French artist, Daumier, showing by what methods the King of Naples restored peace.

London library, the British Museum, a little more than a hundred years ago.

General Haynau escaping with the help of policemen.

Queen Victoria's annoyance with Palmerston increased when she learned that he was receiving some of these refugees, who came to tell him their stories. A climax came when a certain Austrian, General Haynau, visited England. His reputation was known, and it did not endear him to the English. He had behaved with great cruelty in Italy, had ordered the flogging of women and the ill-treatment of prisoners. Always quick to invent a nickname, the English dubbed him General Hyena. During his visit he went to inspect the brewery of Barclay and Perkins, where the indignant draymen, who had heard of his crimes from some Italians working there, seized him and manhandled him so that he had to be rescued by four constables. The Austrian ambassador demanded an apology, which Palmerston gave, but it was an apology with a sting in the tail. He wrote in the letter that he regretted that the General had chosen to visit England when he knew the feeling of the people. This brought an agitated protest from the Queen. Palmerston replied to her at length, and explained that, to the English, General Haynau was on a level with Manning, a man just convicted of a murder, the only difference being that General Haynau had far more victims to his credit than had Mr Manning. Queen Victoria could do nothing against a statesman so much cleverer than herself. It is chiefly due to Palmerston that the Crown did not gain the right to decide our foreign policy.

That does not mean that Palmerston was always right and the Queen and the Prince Consort wrong. Often Palmerston behaved in a rash and even dangerous way. But he was responsible to Parliament, and he could be got rid of if he acted in a way Parliament disapproved of. Whereas the Queen and the Prince were responsible only to themselves, and if they had conducted affairs, there would have been no way of checking them.

The Crimean War

In 1854 Great Britain embarked on one of the most wasteful and most useless wars in our history. There had always been a fear that Russia was a dangerous power, ready to advance into India from the north, and force her way into the Mediterranean through the Dardanelles. British policy was to bolster up Turkey, a country so weak and decaying that it was nicknamed the 'sick man of Europe', in order to prevent Russia from having an outlet to the Mediterranean. If you look at the map you will see how Russia was hemmed in by Turkey, and could not get out of the Black Sea. When war broke out between Russia and Turkey, both Britain and France went to the support of Turkey.

The story of the war is a terrible one, full of confusion and misery. It was forty years since Britain had fought a war, and during that time little attention had been paid to the needs of an army.

Officers used then to buy their commissions, and there was no test of ability or experience. It might happen that a good officer would have to serve under someone who had no qualifications for command, except that he had paid for it. The possession of a commission in peacetime had meant enjoying a privileged position. Officers dressed themselves and their regiments in gorgeous uniforms, and cavalry regiments made a splendid sight when they were reviewed, riding fine horses and going through complicated exercises. But the soldiers were often ill-fed because many officers cheated by taking for themselves part of the money intended for the army food.

So, in 1854, an army with unsuitable officers and ill-fed soldiers embarked for the Crimea, the peninsula in the Black Sea where the war was fought.

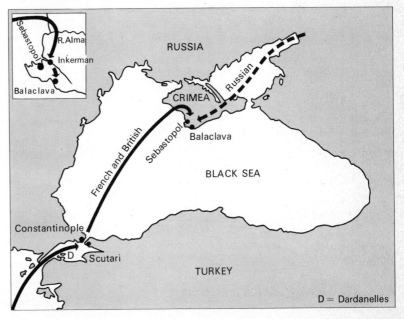

The Russian and the French and British forces advancing to the Crimea. The inset is an enlargement, showing the sites of the battles illustrated on the following pages.

Lord Raglan, the Commander-in-Chief, had fought under Wellington in the Peninsular War and had a great reputation for personal bravery. When, after a battle, his arm had been amputated and thrown into a cart, he had called out 'Bring back my arm, it has my wife's ring on it.' But personal bravery was not enough. He was too old to direct the campaign. For example, he could not always remember that this time we were fighting with the French, not against them, as we had done fifty years before. His orders were confusing because he sometimes referred to the enemy as 'the French'. The most famous example of a muddled order was the one which sent the Light Brigade into an almost certain death; they rode a mile and a half down a valley facing the enemy guns, knowing that only a miracle could save them.

The wife of one of the officers wrote this description of Balaclava, the port where the British supplies were unloaded:

A photograph of Balaclava Harbour taken during the Crimean War. This was the first war to be recorded by photographers, of whom the most important was Roger Fenton.

Winter quarters in the Crimea. William Howard Russell is in the tent *(foreground)*, writing a dispatch to *The Times*.

Florence Nightingale.

If anybody should ever wish to erect a 'model Balaclava' in England, I will tell him the ingredients necessary. Take a village of ruined houses and hovels in the extremest state of all imaginable dirt; allow the rain to pour into and outside them, until the whole place is a swamp of filth ankle deep; catch about, on an average, 1,000 sick Turks with the plague, and cram them into the houses indiscriminately; kill about a hundred a day and bury them so as to be scarcely covered with earth, leaving them to rot at leisure – taking care to keep up the supply. On the one side collect all the exhausted ponies, dying bullocks, and worn-out camels and leave them to die of starvation. They will generally do so in about three days, when they will begin to rot and smell accordingly. Collect together from the water of the harbour all the offal of the animals slaughtered for the use of the above hundred ships, to say nothing of the inhabitants of the town – which together with an occasional floating human body, whole or in parts, and the driftwood of the wrecks, pretty well covers the water – and stew them all up together in a narrow harbour and you will have a tolerable imitation of the real essence of Balaclava.

This was the first war to be reported by the correspondent of a newspaper. William Howard Russell, employed by *The Times*, sent back indignant dispatches, describing how the wounded were neglected. There were not enough medical supplies, not enough doctors and no nurses. If the unfortunate men reached the hospital at Scutari they were sometimes left lying unattended for days because there was a shortage of doctors. An indignant public blamed the government. It was then that Florence Nightingale went out at the request of the government with thirty-eight nurses to look after the wounded in the hospital at Scutari. The story of her fight against all the difficulties which would have overwhelmed a weaker person is one of the most dramatic in our history.

Florence Nightingale came of a rich family and was very handsome. Her family took it for granted that she should spend all her time on social life until she made a good marriage. But she found parties boring, took no interest in social life and longed to be a nurse. Finally, when she was thirty, her parents gave in and allowed her to spend three months at an institution in Germany at Kaiserswerth. It was part orphanage and part hospital. Wherever she had travelled she had visited hospitals, and she had formed the opinion that patients recovered more quickly if they were in well-ventilated wards. After the time at Kaiserswerth she was for a few months in charge of a nursing-home for women in London. She was called in to help with a cholera epidemic at the Middlesex hospital. One of the doctors there noticed how capable she was and asked if she would go there and train nurses. Before this could happen she was asked to go to the Crimea to take charge of the wounded soldiers.

Florence Nightingale hurriedly collected a party of nurses to take with her. When she arrived she found that reports of muddle and confusion were not exaggerated, but with the most extraordinary determination she produced order out of chaos. But one thing she could not do. She could not reduce the death-rate which remained terribly high. Forty per cent of the men brought in died. It was seen that certain beds seemed fatal, soldiers put in them died after two days; this was not surprising since they were placed above faulty drains. Florence Nightingale urged the government to send out a sanitary commission with powers to carry out any necessary work. After she had been there four months, the commission arrived. A proper drainage system was put in and a supply of pure water provided. The death-rate dropped to

Highlanders attacking the Russians at the battle of the Alma.

The charge of the Light
Brigade at Balaclava.

A battery of big guns drawn
up before Sebastopol. The
bombardment lasted eleven
months until the Russians
evacuated the town.

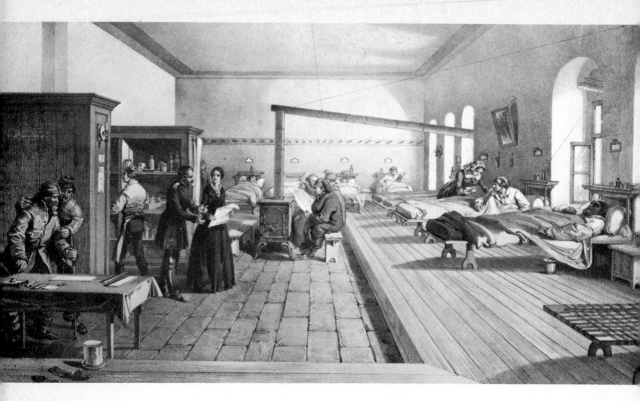

two per cent. This was a proof that bad water and bad drainage were a cause of disease. Exactly how it was caused was not known, but at least the fact had been demonstrated.

On her return from the Crimea, Florence Nightingale organized the first real professional training of nurses. She chose for her hospital St Thomas's, because there was already a good matron there. Nurses went from this school to other hospitals and to organize other training schools, and by the end of the century a revolution had taken place in the care of the sick in hospitals. This change would have come in any case. It was already beginning when Florence Nightingale went to the Crimea, but the reputation she gained there made it possible for the change to come more quickly. She was a national heroine and could speak with authority. By 1900 the stuffy wards, the ignorant nurses, were things of the past.

At the end of the war, when Russia was defeated in 1856, the Sultan of Turkey promised to treat his Christian subjects well, and Russia promised to keep her warships out of the Black Sea. The Sultan of Turkey continued to ill-treat his Christian subjects and a few years later Russia put warships in the Black Sea. John Bright had called the Crimean War 'a crime'.

Palmerston becomes Prime Minister   1855

When the war had been going badly, in 1855, the country had called

Hospital ward at Scutari, showing Florence Nightingale's improvements. The room is light and the windows are open to admit fresh air. The beds are well spaced. Everything looks clean and tidy.

Soldiers working in the Crimean War Cemetery. More than 21,000 British soldiers died in the war.

for Palmerston to be Prime Minister. He kept this position with one short interval until his death ten years later.

He was more popular than ever. He had the credit of having finished the war. His interests were in foreign affairs and, whenever possible, in upholding what he thought were the interests of his country. He was not interested in reforms at home. When he was asked to make some changes he merely laughed and said 'Wait until Gladstone slips into my shoes.' The members of the Cabinet who wanted reform realized that it was hopeless to expect progress; they would have to wait until Gladstone became Prime Minister.

The Chinese ship   1856

In 1856 an opportunity occurred for him to wave the British flag. A Chinese ship called the *Arrow* was seized by the Governor of Canton for piracy and the crew were arrested. Formerly, some years before

European factories in Canton, 1850.

this, the *Arrow* had sailed under the British Flag; then it had been sold to a Chinese merchant. The Englishman who was in charge of our trading interests in the East asked for the release of the men. Palmerston rushed to support this demand, and ordered the bombardment of Canton. The Chinese had no chance against the formidable power of the British, and the defences of Canton were destroyed with great loss of life.

There were many members of the House of Commons, on both sides, Liberals and Conservatives, who strongly disapproved of such a high-handed and illegal action. Gladstone, Disraeli, Russell and Bright led an attack on Palmerston and he was defeated on a vote of confidence. He immediately dissolved Parliament and called for a general election. The voters were so dazzled by his speeches during this campaign when he spoke of the insult to our flag, and called the Chinese 'insolent barbarians', that he was returned with a substantial majority.

The American Civil War   1861–5

In 1861 war broke out between the northern and the southern states of America. A northern ship stopped a British liner, which was carrying two unofficial delegates from the southern states. The American captain transferred the two men to his own ship and took them to New York. Palmerston drafted a letter to President Lincoln, in protest against searching a British ship, a letter which was couched in such intemperate language that it would have been difficult for the President to persuade his people not to declare war on Britain. Fortunately the Prince Consort saw this draft and altered it before it was sent. This was almost the Prince's last action. He died at the end of the year.

The American Civil War: an artillery unit of northerners pose for Mathew Brady, an American photographer who became famous for his war photographs.

Death of the Prince Consort

The Prince died in December 1861. The court became quieter than ever. Queen Victoria continued to mourn for him; for many years she wore deep black and refused to open Parliament or to carry out any of her ordinary duties. She was determined to do whatever the Prince would have wished. She only lived, she said, to carry on his work. This withdrawal from public life made her unpopular, especially when she sent messages to Parliament, asking that her children, as one by one they married, should be granted an income from the state. There were even some suggestions that a republic would be better than such an expensive monarchy.

The Queen and the Prince Consort had been strict and unimaginative parents. This was particularly the case with the Prince of Wales (afterwards Edward VII). They were so anxious that he should be trained to be a good king that he was overburdened with work, and subjected to daily lectures on his duty.

Queen Victoria would never allow her son to help her with her work, or to see the state papers, and learn how the country was run. She kept the reins in her own hands. All her ministers, in turn, suggested that the Prince should be given some responsible job. Queen Victoria was adamant. The Prince must not be allowed to do anything except attend functions such as opening hospitals.

We shall read later how Disraeli coaxed her out of her retirement.

Dates to remember

1848   The 'year of revolutions'
1854–6   Crimean War
1861–5   The American Civil War

Things to do

1   Find out the meaning of 'Gunboat Diplomacy'.
2   What was 'the thin red line'?
3   What three garments do we associate with the Crimean War?
4   Find out the causes of the American Civil War.
5   Find out about early war photographers, in particular Roger Fenton and Mathew Brady.

Things to discuss

Palmerston called the Chinese 'barbarians'. Do you think he knew much about them?

Books to read

Garth Lean, *Brave Men Choose,* Blandford
C. Woodham-Smith, *The Reason Why,* Penguin
C. Woodham-Smith, *Lady-in-Chief: Florence Nightingale,* Methuen

Chapter 6
Railways and the Great Exhibition

At the time of the Roman occupation of Britain a Roman officer could travel from Rome to Londinium in three weeks. In the year 1840 it took one of Queen Victoria's ministers eleven days to get back to London from Rome. Nearly 1,800 years had gone by, and the travelling had only been reduced by ten days. Now the journey is done by air in two and a half hours.

Travel by coach

It is only in the last 150 years that travel has been easy, comfortable and safe. Before that time people travelled as little as possible, most of them not at all. By 1800 road surfaces had been so much improved that coaches could rattle along them quickly, and no longer were the unlucky travellers hurled into the ditch when the coach fell into a rut. Coaching is now made to sound romantic. We think of the postboy blowing his horn and the horses clattering down the street, and the old inns where they stopped to change horses. It was probably not so

A stage coach travelling between London and Brighton in 1822.

romantic as Christmas cards make it appear. For one thing it must have been extremely cold outside and extremely stuffy inside. However, the coaches solved the problem of people going from one town to another.

But a much more important problem for an industrial country like Britain was to get goods carried quickly. Canals had been built in the eighteenth century. They were used for transporting heavy and bulky goods. It was a slow method and in any case there remained large parts of the country where it was impossible to build them.

Rails made for carrying coal

The most important commodity was coal. It cost time and labour to dig the coal, but it was even more costly to transport it from the mine after it had been dug out. It was loaded on to carts drawn by horses and conveyed to the nearest waterway or seaport. Coal was shipped from Newcastle to London on colliers, as the boats were called. By the time it reached London the price was six times as high as it had been at the pithead.

It was hard work for the horses to drag the load over uneven ground, so they laid rails down, which made it possible for the cart to be pulled along smoothly. It was reckoned that by this method one horse could do the work that previously eight had done. At first the rails were made like tramlines; then they found that the coaldust got into the grooves, so they raised the rails and put a flange on the edge of the wagon wheels. This meant that the width of all the carts must be absolutely alike to fit the rails. By accident it happened in Newcastle, where this method was first used, that the space between the wheels was exactly four feet eight and a half inches, and that is the exact measurement of our railway lines today.

Soon there was a network of these lines round every pithead.

The use of steam

George Stephenson was the first man to think that an engine instead of a horse might be used to draw the coal-trucks. Since he was a boy of nine he had worked in the mines. He experimented with locomotives and built a line from Stockton to Darlington, on which trucks were drawn by steam engines instead of horses. This is sometimes called the first railway line, but it was not a railway in the modern sense. It belonged to the company for which Stephenson worked and was used to haul their coal. Horses still continued to be used on it as well as locomotives, and passengers were seldom carried on it.

The first railway opened   1830

Nevertheless it was this first attempt that began the railway boom. Enterprising citizens in Lancashire subscribed to form a company to build a line from Manchester to Liverpool, a distance of twenty-nine miles. Stephenson was given the job of designing it. The reaction of the

Stage coach driver.

public seems odd to us today. There were many prophets of doom. Most people are nervous of anything startlingly new. The idea that there could be a substitute for the horse seemed outlandish to many, and the cost was so enormous that people were sure the investors would lose their money. The total cost was £820,000, a great sum in those days. One doctor said that going through the air at such a rate would cause the human frame to collapse (this was at a time when no engine had done more than fifteen miles an hour). Farmers complained that the noise would terrify the cattle, and the cows would give no milk. Housewives objected to the smoke. One suggestion made was that on both sides of the line a wall should be built fifteen feet high to prevent people from being frightened by the sight of a train. The Duke of

Behind this miner at the pithead a steam engine is drawing trucks of coal along a rail track.

Early passenger train, with closed coaches, for the rich.

Liverpool Station 1831.

Early passenger train, with open carriages, charging lower fares.

Wellington was very much against this idea of a railway; he said it would enable the lower classes to move about, and he thought this undesirable.

Stephenson carried on with his work in spite of all the criticisms and objections. We have to remember that at this time there were neither technical schools nor engineering handbooks. The engineers who worked on these first railways were pioneers, who learned by doing the work. Stephenson had the problem of tunnelling and of making the line across a piece of marshy land called Chat Moss. The ground was so spongy that no one could tread on it, yet he had to lay a line firm enough for a heavy train to drive over it. People at that day thought it was like a miracle, and when we look back on it now, we are inclined to

agree with them. After four years and many miscalculations, from which later railway builders learned, in 1830, this first Manchester to Liverpool line was completed.

The opening was magnificent. The Duke of Wellington was there (in spite of his general disapproval), twelve peers of the realm, two ambassadors, and 50,000 spectators. The carriages were shaped like the old horse coaches and there were also trucks for the less important people to travel in. These had no sides or roof, so you can understand that to sit in an open truck and to be whirled along at an unheard-of speed was frightening to some of the passengers. Altogether 800 people were seated in this first train. Fanny Kemble wrote:

The most intense excitement and curiosity prevailed, and though the weather was uncertain, enormous masses of densely packed people lined the road, shouting and waving hats and handkerchiefs, as we flew by them. What with the sight and sound of these cheering multitudes and the tremendous velocity with which we were borne past them, my spirits rose to champagne height, and I never enjoyed anything so much as the first hour of our progress.

The tremendous speed of which Fanny Kemble wrote was thirty miles an hour. That was faster than anyone had dreamed possible. One thing only spoilt the success of the day. Huskisson was killed when he stepped from the train at a station and was knocked down by an engine, the 'Rocket', coming from the opposite direction.

The railway boom 1838–48

This successful venture started the big railway boom. Everywhere groups of men raised the capital to build railways. The first ones were all short stretches, such as Leeds to York, Newcastle to Carlisle, Canterbury to Whitstable. It was about ten years before the idea of long distance trains arose. Before any line was built there had to be approval by Parliament (in one year there were 262 railway bills presented to the House of Commons), the land had to be surveyed and then had to be bought. Here the companies often found difficulties. Some towns which were on a direct line refused to have the railway (much to their later regret). Cambridge insisted that the station should be a long way from the town. The authorities there were afraid the students might be tempted to travel to London. The landowners could ask what price they liked, since there were no compulsory purchase orders at that time. If a landowner knew that his land was particularly desirable he would put up the price. One bit of land which was valued at £5,500 was sold for £120,000. This made the building of railways more expensive than it need have been, and it is not surprising that some companies had to go bankrupt, though most of them did well, and were able to pay a ten per cent dividend to their subscribers. So railway investment was a popular one. If you look at the maps you will see how quickly Britain was covered with railway lines.

George Hudson, the 'Railway King'. By 1840 he had amalgamated under his control more than 1,000 miles of railway. But his company eventually went bankrupt.

1839

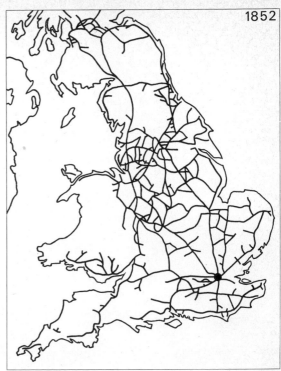

1852

Darlington to
Stockton 1825

Liverpool to
Manchester
1830

London to
Birmingham
1838

Railways developed rapidly
in the thirteen years between
1839–52.

Brunel and the broad gauge

An engineer even more remarkable than Stephenson was Isambard
Kingdom Brunel, the son of a French refugee, who was also an engineer
and who had begun to construct the first tunnel under the Thames. The
son helped his father in this and then turned his attention to the design
of locomotives and to railways. He was responsible for the Great Western
Railway from London to Bristol, and he also built the first steamship to
cross the Atlantic. Brunel's lines had a wider gauge; they were seven
feet across. He argued that a broad gauge would not only be more comfortable but quicker and safer, and he won his point. The Great Western
engines travelled at sixty miles an hour and the coaches were roomy and
comfortable, with less vibration than on the narrow gauge railways.
A bitter battle was fought over this and in the end the narrow gauge
won, because there were already so many miles of narrow gauge and it
would have been expensive to alter it. At that time if you travelled by
the Great Western you could not take a train which ran through on to
another line because of the different gauge and for this reason the broad
gauge was finally given up.

When you travel by train do you ever notice the embankments and
the tunnels and wonder how they were made? There were no mechanical
devices then, such as bulldozers. The work was all done by back-
breaking labour. First the surveyors would map out a route. A train
could not travel up an incline, nor could it run round a sharp curve,

89

and as there is comparatively little flat land, tunnels and viaducts had to be built.

When the surveyors had finished their work, contractors were given the job of preparing the track. They hired gangs of 'navvies' (short for navigators) who had to blast through rock and dig up the earth. These navvies became a legend of toughness and strength. They were reputed to drink a gallon of beer and eat two pounds of beef a day. Because the contractors knew they would lose money if the work were delayed, they were often inclined to hurry it on without heeding the danger. Accidents were frequent when blasting and tunnelling were in progress. The navvies came from Ireland and Scotland and the north of England. Erse and Gaelic, as well as the accents of Dublin and Glasgow were heard in the English countryside.

Imagine the effect on a peaceful village, whose inhabitants had never travelled more than a few miles to the nearest market town, when a thousand navvies came and camped in the fields. The clergy preached against them. The landlords feared them. The mothers warned their daughters against them. They drank and fought and poached. But they built Britain's railways and so laid the foundations of British prosperity. They strutted round on Sunday wearing tall white hats, red plush waistcoats and moleskin breeches.

The dangers inherent in their work led, as in the case of miners or soldiers during a war, to a feeling of comradeship amongst them. There

Clifton Suspension Bridge over the Avon Gorge, Bristol, designed by Brunel.

was no compensation from the contractors for any injury. Though the clergy might condemn them as a lot of immoral and brutal men, they helped each other and would take up a collection for anyone who was hurt. They did not poach on Lord Harewood's estate because Lady Harewood had been kind to them.

When the first railway was built in France, 5,000 British navvies were shipped across to build it. They were sent to the Crimea to make a railway there. They went to Canada, South Africa and South America. So while we rightly do homage to the great engineers such as Stephenson and Brunel, we should remember also the navvies who made these engineering marvels possible.

Then when the line was completed the villagers would see the famous iron horse, puffing and snorting down the line. The engine-drivers and firemen were skilled workers and were also better paid than labourers. A local West country song gives this warning:

Come all you young maidens, take warning from me
    Shun all engine firemen and their company:
He'll tell you he loves you and all kinds of lies,
    But the one that he loves is the train that he drives.

I once loved a fireman and he said he loved me
    He took me a-walking in to the country
He hugged me and kissed me and gazed in my eyes
    And said 'You're as nice as the eight forty-five'.

A sailor comes home when his voyage is done
    A soldier gets weary of following the drum
A collier will cleave to his loved one, for life
    But a fireman's one love is the engine, his wife.

A navvy.

Though the idea of railways had first been to carry goods, the companies found they could make a profit out of carrying passengers too. Parliament passed an act in 1844 which said that at least one train a day must stop at every station and that the rate for third-class travel must be a penny a mile. This act also laid down that all carriages must have sides. Travelling grew more comfortable as one by one improvements were made, and also safer brakes were invented so that accidents became fewer. The prejudice against railway travel died down quickly. We find one lady, Mrs Trollope, who, when she came to London, always stopped at a station outside the town and then drove in a horse carriage to London. She did not want her fashionable friends to know that she had sat in a railway carriage amongst strangers. But at last even the Mrs Trollopes got over this objection. Third-class carriages were not at first put on all trains, but when it was found that it was profitable because of the numbers of travellers, they were attached to fast as well as slow trains. Not until the end of the century was there any heating in the trains, though oil lamps for lighting were provided.

At first the trains were not punctual. You would go hopefully to a station and might have to wait a long time before a train appeared. Then a man called Bradshaw edited a timetable book for the convenience of passengers, and the railway companies were indignant. They said the public would now expect the trains to run at the time they were advertised.

Benefits brought by railways

Not everybody profited from the railways. Those who had their money in canals were ruined; the canals soon became neglected and derelict. The owners of coaches were also out of pocket, and the inns where horses had been changed lost their prosperity and turned into ordinary country public houses. The main roads were now deserted; they did not come back to life until motor-cars were invented.

Who gained most from the railways? First of all the manufacturers.

A London railway station of 1874, with two familiar features: advertising posters covering the walls and the W. H. Smith newspaper stall (*right*). An expanding system of railways made it possible to distribute newspapers quickly over a wide area.

THE PICTURESQUE
COSTUMES OF
SCOTLAND
AS WORN BY THE
ROYAL PRINCES
Kilt Suits for fishing & Shooting
Full Dress for Evening wear
BOYS HIGHLAND DRESSES.
WATERPROOF
Overcoats for DEER STALKING.
JOHN T.W. GOODMAN, TAILOR
5 LITTLE ARGYLL ST. REGENT ST.

SHERRY.
FREE FROM ACIDITY OR HEAT.
SOLE IMPORTERS,
30/-
CONDUIT STREET, LONDON,
MANCHESTER & BRIGHTON.

TRADE MARK.
COUGH LOZENGES
BEST & SAFEST REMEDY.
OF ALL CHEMISTS.
BOXES 1S 1½ AND 2S 9D

CHAPEL STREET
WEST
CURZON STREET
MAYFAIR.

LAMPLOUGH'S PYRETIC SALINE IS PLEASANT & CURES HEADACHE
SICKNESS, BILIOUSNESS & SKIN AFFECTIONS

RAILWAY, & GENERAL
ACCIDENT
INSURANCE COMPANY,
LIMITED
AGAINST ALL KINDS OF ACCIDENTS
BY LAND AND SEA.

JOHN BRINSMEAD & SONS
ON THE
GOLD MEDAL
THREE YEARS SYSTEM PIANOS.
18 WIGMORE ST.
LONDON, W.

BURGLAR-PROOF SAFES.
FIRE-RESISTING SAFES.
CHATWOOD,
Is the only maker of Safes who allows Thirty-six hours Test with
any kind of Burglar's appliances before delivery.
120, CANNON STREET, LONDON. E.C.

W.H.SMITH & SON
186, STRAND.

Coal could now be brought quickly and cheaply, so that a factory did not have to be built as near as possible to a mine. This meant that goods were produced more cheaply, prices fell, and when that happened the demand for goods went up because more people could afford to buy them. Business was also helped by the increased speed. The penny post had been established and letters were sent by train; a businessman could rely on a speedy reply and appointments could be kept more punctually.

Railways created a new industry of their own. Not only were thousands engaged in building the lines, but thousands more were employed in making the rails and the engines and all the other parts of a train. And they were doing this not only for England but also for countries abroad. English engines were sold in Belgium, France and Germany. British firms constructed railways in India, Canada and South America; Britain became the engineering centre of the world.

Left: The site of King's Cross Station, 1832. Stations had to be constructed on the edge of cities and towns where large enough areas of land were available. Stations such as St Pancras and Euston were at this time outside London.

Below: Metropolitan Railway, King's Cross Station in about 1863.

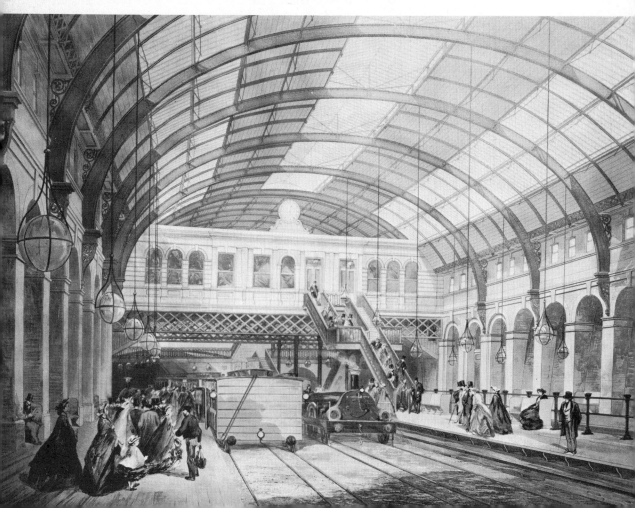

Railway accident near Beckenham, Kent, in January 1866, caused by the collapse of the bridge.

All over the world, when there were railways to be built, you would find the British engineer laying British rails and the profits went into the pocket of the British ironmaster.

The shopkeeper in the small town gained too. His goods could be promptly delivered. The big towns no longer had to rely for their food on the country immediately surrounding them. Before this, droves of sheep and cattle used to be driven into the towns to be slaughtered there in the butchers' shops. This custom had made the streets dirty and had produced nauseating smells. Fresh meat could not have been dispatched to the towns before there were railways. Cows, too, had been kept in towns in stalls and milked there. Many people living in inland towns had never tasted fresh sea fish. The railways, too, changed the size of towns which could now expand without fear of food shortage. They also changed the shape of the towns, for more workers were brought in for the new industries and the richer people now moved out to suburbs some five or six miles from their place of business. They could travel into work by train and so the centre of the town was left for the poorer city dweller.

What about the travelling public? The middle-class people began their habit of a yearly seaside holiday. This caused the development of places like Eastbourne and Bournemouth from little fishing villages to seaside places with rows of boarding houses and hotels. This holiday trade provided seasonal work for many people.

The Factory Act of 1847 gave a free Saturday afternoon, and later still four days a year, called Bank Holidays, were granted. Cheap excursions enabled thousands of city dwellers to go for a day to the unspoilt country or to the seaside, and the country dwellers had a chance to see the marvels of the town.

The Great Exhibition   1851

The Crystal Palace.

One person in England who appreciated the value of all the mechanical inventions was Prince Albert, the Queen's husband. He thought of organizing an international exhibition of all the new machines and processes, believing that it would stimulate trade. He called together a few scientific men who were interested and formed a committee to carry out the project. They decided to hold the exhibition in Hyde Park.

For a long time the scheme was regarded as a huge joke. The comic papers made continual jibes at the expense of the committee. Then when it was known that trees would have to be cut down in Hyde Park in order to put up a building to house all the exhibits, there was a storm of protest. The gardener of the Duke of Devonshire, a man called Paxton, suggested that he should put up a structure made of panes of glass, like the large greenhouses he had built at Chatsworth, the home

'Albert, spare those trees!' In this cartoon from *Punch*, Colonel Sibthorp, an opponent of the Great Exhibition plans, is trying to stop the Prince Consort from cutting down trees on the Hyde Park site.

of the Duke of Devonshire. The Prince persuaded the committee to accept this plan. It had the great advantage that no trees would have to be cut down. The glass walls would tower over the tops of the trees. When the building was near completion someone exclaimed 'Why, it is a palace of crystal,' and the name 'Crystal Palace' stuck.

Most people were sceptical about the whole undertaking, just as they had been sceptical about a locomotive ever doing the work of a horse. The Prince plodded on in spite of all the gloomy prophecies he heard on all sides. London, said some, would be overrun with foreign pickpockets, thieves and murderers; a great horde from the provinces would swarm into town and ransack the houses. One paper went further and said there would be a general insurrection accompanied by much bloodshed. In any case, people thought a glass building would not be strong enough to hold the heavy machinery, and one man said that the vibration from guns which would fire the salute would shatter the whole edifice and cause it to fall down on innocent spectators. It is difficult to understand why people were so pessimistic. Perhaps one reason was that the Prince had never been popular in England. He was regarded as a foreigner and Englishmen tended to look on foreigners with suspicion.

In the meantime the railways saw their chance. They announced cheap fares and excursions from all parts of the country to see the great sight. This meant for the Londoners another prospect of ruin. Not many years before they had watched troops and guns being sent north to quell the Chartists, and thought of northerners as uncivilized and dangerous. Now would all these northern hordes descend on peaceful London?

However much people might sneer, they were all curious, and for opening day, 1 May 1851, all the 2,500 tickets were sold out at a price of three guineas for a man and two guineas for a woman. It happened to be a particularly bright sunny day. From early morning crowds assembled near Hyde Park to watch the royal family arrive. Many country families had driven in their carriages to Hyde Park and had camped by the roadside in Piccadilly. They could be seen eating their breakfast, cooked by footmen on portable stoves. Humbler people brought sandwiches. Small boys hung on trees, like a crop of apples, and defied all efforts to dislodge them. Punctually the Queen, the Prince and their two eldest children appeared and the Great Exhibition was opened by a performance of the Hallelujah Chorus sung by the combined choirs of the Chapel Royal, Westminster Abbey, St Paul's, Windsor, and the Sacred Harmonic School, accompanied by the organ of 4,260 pipes specially built for the occasion. Then the 2,500 visitors went round to inspect the exhibits. Most of the objects were British, though some foreign firms had sent specimens. There could be seen all the newest products, machines, tools, fabrics, furniture, silver and glassware, porcelain, everything in fact which was made in England.

So on they came, all through the summer. They streamed in from the trains which unloaded them in London, workers from the Midlands

Papiermâché chair shown at the Exhibition.

Drawing-room table from the Exhibition.

and the north, rustics from the villages. The entrance fee was reduced four days a week to a shilling. By the end of the season 6,200,000 people had visited the Great Exhibition; 75,000 of them had been foreigners. And not one of those dreadful warnings had been necessary. Far from being robbed, the Londoners had made a lot of money out of the visitors. There were no riots; everyone commented on the orderly behaviour of the crowds. They did not even pick the flowers in the park, nor did they break into houses. The world gasped and admired, and those who had sneered at the Prince Consort had to eat their words. What had happened? An unprecedented number of people had seen the ingenuity, the skill and craftsmanship of the British. It had been from beginning to end a triumphant success. It had also made a considerable profit. This profit was used to set up in Kensington a college to teach the new sciences. Since that time Kensington has been a home of scientific training.

Is it any wonder that the British – looking at this exhibition – felt proud and superior? Is it surprising that when they travelled abroad they swaggered and boasted? British industry had created this new world. The idea of an exhibition was copied in France by the Emperor Napoleon III who held two similar ones in Paris.

The Crystal Palace was dismantled and re-erected at Sydenham on a hill, and was a landmark for many miles. In 1936 it was accidentally burnt down. There must have been a very few old people alive then who could have remembered as small children seeing the marvellous Crystal Palace in all its glory.

Dates to Remember

1830   Manchester to Liverpool railway opened
1844   The first steamship crossed the Atlantic
1851   The Great Exhibition

Things to do

1 Draw a map of your town and the surroundings, about fifteen miles in each direction. Put in the railway lines and stations, and find out why the stations were built in those particular places.

2 Find out how many old coaching inns you have in the neighbourhood. You can recognize them by the wide archway leading into the stable-yard where the coach could be turned round. If you know of any public houses called 'The Navigator' or 'The Navigators' Arms' find out when and why they were given their names.

3 What other exhibitions have you heard about either in England or in any other country?

4 What advantages came to Britain from the Great Exhibition?

Interesting people to read about: George Stephenson and Isambard Kingdom Brunel. There are many books about Queen Victoria. Ask in your library if they have any of the catalogues of the Great Exhibition.

Books to read

Terry Coleman, *The Railway Navvies*, Hutchinson
R. Manning-Sanders, *Seaside England*, Batsford
H. C. B. Rogers, *From Turnpike to Iron Road*, Seeley
R. J. Salter, *Isambard Kingdom Brunel*, Lutterworth
J. B. Snell, *Early Railways*, Weidenfeld & Nicolson
R. B. Way, *The Story of British Locomotives*, Methuen

Come all you young maidens, take warning from me Shun all en-gine firemen and their com-pa- ny; He'll tell you he loves you and all kinds of lies, But the one that he loves is the train that he drives.

Chapter 7
Politics   1867–1900

The age of prosperity   1846–80

In the years following the repeal of the Corn Laws from 1846–80
fortune smiled on Great Britain. On Tyneside and the Clyde there was
a constant hammering as the ships which were to carry British goods
to the far corners of the earth were being built. They carried cotton
goods to the East and brought back silks, spices and tea, and the
profits – substantial ones – rolled into the pockets of the British
businessmen. What was the cause of all this prosperity? A manufacturer
has normally two problems. He must know how to make his goods and
then find somewhere to sell them. The British manufacturer had had

long experience in making things; his goods were better than those made by any other country. The world wanted to buy them because they were cheap. There was no need to scout for customers; the customers were lined up and waiting. Why were the goods so cheap? It was because the raw materials came in free from customs duties; we had in this country a limitless supply of coal and iron, so that provided we had the cotton, wool, timber and other materials we needed, we could make what the world wanted at a low price. Food was cheap, therefore wages bought more goods. The cheaper things are, the more will be sold, and the more sold, the greater the profit. With these profits the manufacturer could increase the size of his factory or build a new one. This meant that the building industry flourished.

The middle-classes began to build themselves fine houses and fill them with expensive furniture, so the towns expanded and penetrated further into the country. The towns became smokier; in some places it seemed as if people were living in a perpetual fog. In the Midlands the blast furnaces from the iron foundries lit up the sky at night. Ugly

The 'black country' round Wolverhampton.

slag heaps appeared where there had once been woods and fields. This was the price paid for the boom in trade. 'Where there's muck, there's money' was the saying then.

Even poor boys grew rich. Ruskin's father came to London as a junior clerk in a wine merchant's office. After thirty years he was an extremely wealthy man. A popular book at the time was *Self Help*, written by Samuel Smiles. He set out to prove how a poor man by thrift and energy could become rich and independent. He gave suggestions as to how a man should invest his savings even if they were only a penny a day. He preached self-denial and explained how a glass of beer a day would cost 45s. a year, and for that sum a man might insure his life for £130, payable at death. He made it clear to his readers that if anyone were not prosperous, that was because he was not thrifty.

The two great English statesmen of these years were Gladstone and Disraeli.

William Ewart Gladstone.

Gladstone

Gladstone, who led the Liberal Party, came from a rich Liverpool merchant family. He had the usual education of that class, Eton and Oxford, and when he was young he wanted to become a clergyman. His father opposed this idea and persuaded him instead to take a seat in the House of Commons. He worked there with intense seriousness and spoke of his appointment as Prime Minister as a 'mission'. Unlike Palmerston, he was not interested in bullying other countries. He wanted peace and he thought that if wars were avoided the country would become more and more prosperous. He believed that the National Debt could be wiped out in a few years.

As a young man he had once visited Naples, and the sights that he saw there had a deep effect on his policy. The King of Naples had just arrested a group of liberals who wanted reforms in the government. Gladstone had permission to visit them, and the degrading conditions of the prisons and the sufferings of those men were something he remembered all his life. He always wanted to help any nation which was struggling for its freedom. He was an exact and conscientious man, who did not believe in wasting either time or money. On his honeymoon, while he and his bride were travelling, if they had to wait at a station he would bring out a copy of Homer, his favourite Greek poet, and study it. We are not told what his bride did; probably she just had to look at the railway track. His wife was a delightful woman, who was untidy, unpunctual and not very good at accounts.

Unfortunately he was not able to see another person's point of view. If anyone differed from him, Gladstone thought it must be due to wilfulness. Even the members of his own cabinet could not discuss freely with him. He gave the orders and they had to follow them. His worst trouble was with Queen Victoria. He had a tremendous respect for her, but he wearied her with long explanations which she could not understand. He thought it was his duty to explain everything to

Cartoon of the House of
Commons, 1849. Disraeli is
on the right, conspicuous in
his checked trousers. The
'blue books' lying on the floor
contain parliamentary reports.

her. Once when there was a particularly complicated bill, he sent what
he called a short summary of it. The short summary was twelve closely-
written pages. Poor Queen Victoria threw it away in despair. She could
not understand a word of it. Gladstone did not realize that other people
might not be interested in his closely-reasoned arguments. Once he
spoke in the House of Commons for eight hours.

Disraeli

His opponent, Disraeli, was as unlike him as any man could be. He
was born into a Jewish family, although baptized as a Christian, and
did not go to any public school or university. He had no influential
friends to help him on in life. When he was first elected to Parliament
he determined to make himself noticed. He certainly was. When he
rose to speak for the first time he was dressed in an elaborately coloured
waistcoat and an embroidered coat and wore diamond rings. His speech
was greeted with jeers and boos. He continued with it, though not a
single sentence was heard. The next day the members felt a little
ashamed of the way they had behaved and this time they listened to
him. Soon everyone looked forward to hearing him, because he proved
to be a witty speaker, and a most dangerous opponent. He could turn on
sarcasm and make an unfortunate member writhe. Gradually he gained
the confidence of the Conservative Party, and its leader, Peel, was
especially kind to him. You remember that the Tory party was split

103

over the repeal of the Corn Laws, and that Disraeli made a cruel attack on his old friend Peel on that occasion. Disraeli set to work to build up the section of the Tories which supported protection and therefore deserted Peel, into a new, powerful, imperialist Conservative party. As a part of this policy he wanted to make the monarchy interesting and popular.

He did one thing which Gladstone could never do. He won the affection of Queen Victoria. He was an expert in flattery. He said once to a friend that when it came to royalty you had 'to put it on with a trowel.' Her sad face – she lived a gloomy life after the death of the Prince Consort – used to light up when Disraeli talked to her, his 'Fairy Queen' as he called her. This was when she was a middle-aged and portly woman, so the term 'laying it on with a trowel' was hardly an exaggeration. On one occasion she sent him some primroses and in his letter of thanks he wrote 'truly they are more precious than rubies, coming as they do from the sovereign he adores.' Disraeli, like Gladstone, was very happily married. His wife, who was twelve years older than he was himself, was rather a ridiculous figure, and made tactless remarks. But no one dared show any amusement when Disraeli was there. He adored his Mary Ann.

Disraeli introduced the second Reform Act into the House of Commons in 1867. This act gave the vote to all householders in the towns, whatever their incomes. He was Prime Minister for a few months in 1868, and hoped that the new voters would support him at the next election, but they were most of them members of the working-class and preferred the Liberal to the Conservative Party. The next year the Liberals won the election and became the government for six years. After that, in 1874, the Conservatives won an election and it was their turn to rule for six years.

Although people at the time saw these two parties as opposed to each other in everything, if we look at the acts passed during these two long ministries we shall not see so very much difference in the policy of each party. Gladstone's attention was fixed a great deal of the time on Ireland, which will be discussed in another chapter. He was concerned with making the government efficient and bringing it up to date; he began the system of giving posts in the Civil Service on the results of examinations, instead of just handing them over to some relation or friend of a member of Parliament; he also brought in the act which made it necessary for army officers to pass an examination. No longer could the soldiers be led by men who had no knowledge at all of military matters. Both these acts were resented by the people who had hoped to find convenient posts for their sons, but he argued that the country could not afford the old haphazard system whereby idle young men could have comfortable jobs with a good salary and not much work.

Disraeli's 'Fairy Queen'.

Liberal reforms 1868–74

The Secret Ballot Act was passed. This had been one of the points of

By-election at Taunton, 1873. This was one of the first to be held after the Secret Ballot Act had been passed. The votes were put in the box on the table.

the People's Charter. After this no one could know how a man voted, and he could not suffer in his job if he happened to vote against his employer or his landlord. An act was passed to enable the Trade Unions to be registered as Friendly Societies. This was needed because in the past if a Trade Union official had misused the money in his care, the Trade Union could not sue him, because it was not what was called a 'recognized society'. Another important measure was the Education Act, which will be explained in another chapter.

In international affairs Gladstone was true to his principles of justice. During the Civil War in America, we had remained neutral. In spite of this, the government had connived at the building of a Confederate battleship called the *Alabama* in the Liverpool dockyard. This ship had done a great deal of damage to the northerners who now demanded compensation. Gladstone admitted the justice of this claim, although the country was indignant at the idea of giving in to another nation. He proposed that the matter should be submitted to international arbitration. The committee met in Geneva, the first time that city was used for an international meeting, and it was decided that Britain should pay £3,000,000. There was a howl of rage from many people in the country but Gladstone faced that calmly. Opinion about the *Alabama* claim was one of the reasons for Gladstone's defeat at the next election. Another unpopular measure which influenced the voters was the Licensing Act, which restricted the hours when public houses could be opened.

Conservative measures   1874–80

Disraeli now had six years in office. Queen Victoria heaved a sigh of relief. For six years she had been forced to sign bills of which she disapproved, as well as having to listen to long and tiresome speeches from a minister whom she did not like. Now she could sit back and relax, soothed and flattered. Disraeli knew how to please her. He suggested that she should take the title of Empress of India, and it was with pride that she signed herself Victoria R and I, to stand for Victoria, Queen and Empress. When Disraeli, on behalf of Britain, bought half the shares in the Suez Canal (he wanted to have control of the route to India), he made it appear as a personal present to the Queen. 'You have it, Madam,' he said. 'It is yours.' He left most of the questions of reform to his Home Secretary, Mr Cross, who did excellent work. It was due to him that Medical Officers were appointed in all districts, and councils given power over slum clearance. The last of the children were freed, the climbing boys, or chimney-sweeps. This act which forbade the employment of the climbing boys was only passed after two dreadful deaths had occurred, one of them the death of a little boy of five who had died of suffocation a quarter of an hour after he was sent up a chimney. Another act was passed as a result of a member losing his temper. A man called Samuel Plimsoll had for a long

'New crowns for old ones!' Disraeli, represented in this *Punch* cartoon as an eastern wizard, presents the crown of India to Queen Victoria.

Opening of the Suez Canal in 1869.

A *Punch* cartoon of Disraeli, who, by buying shares in the Suez Canal, gained control of the quick route to India. The Sphinx looks on with approval.

time concerned himself with the plight of the merchant seaman. They often had to sail in unseaworthy or overloaded boats. The owners knew they would get insurance money if the ships came to grief. The men called them 'coffin ships'. Several times Plimsoll had tried to introduce a bill on this subject. Always the House of Commons had no time to discuss it. Then Plimsoll lost his temper and shouted 'You're a lot of damned murderers.' The members were shocked at the language but they were also shocked at the truth of the statement. An act was passed ordering a line to be drawn round every ship, to show how much it could safely be loaded. You can always see this Plimsoll line on a ship.

The Trade Unionists were struggling to get the law against picketing in a strike abolished. Picketing means persuading blacklegs not to take the jobs of the strikers. There had been a strike in the Durham coalfields, where the blacklegs had been roughly handled. The local song with its hidden threat in the last verse showed the feelings of the miners.

> Oh every evening after dark,
> The blackleg miners creep to work,
> With corduroys and coaly shirt,
> The dirty blackleg miners.
>
> They take their picks and down they go,
> To dig the coal that lies below,
> And there isn't a woman in all the town
> Would look at a blackleg miner.
>
> So join the union while you may,
> Don't wait until your dying day,
> For that may not be far away
> You dirty blackleg miner.

Benjamin Disraeli.

Disraeli's Act said that peaceful picketing was legal; this meant that persuasion, but not physical force, was allowed. It also freed the Trade Unionists from the fear that they might be prosecuted for conspiracy if they entered on a strike. This act laid down that if any act was lawful for one person to do, it was also lawful for a combination of persons, for example, a Trade Union, to do it.

Disraeli was forceful in foreign policy. He believed that Great Britain should interfere when other countries seemed to threaten our interests. In 1877 Russia defeated Turkey and forced the Sultan to set up an independent state of Bulgaria. Disraeli was immediately alarmed. This might increase the influence of Russia in eastern Europe. He demanded that a conference of the powers should be summoned in Berlin. They met under the chairmanship of the German Chancellor, Bismarck. The treaty which Russia had made was altered and a new one, the Treaty of Berlin, was agreed to. By this, a large part of Bulgaria was given back to Turkey, and Cyprus was handed over to Britain. Austria was made protector over two of the Balkan States. By these means Disraeli hoped to curb the power of Russia. He came home in triumph, saying that he had brought back 'Peace with Honour'. It was due to this fear of Russia that an expedition was sent into Afghanistan, because Disraeli thought Russia was trying to penetrate into India.

In 1880 he was defeated in the general election and Queen Victoria had to say farewell to her favourite minister.

The organization of business

Improvements were made in the design of the machines and they grew more costly as they grew more intricate. It became increasingly difficult for a factory-owner to find all the capital to keep his business up to date. He could invite people to buy shares in his firm. This could be risky, and although a fortune might be made, if the business failed a fortune might be lost. Cautious people invested their savings in the government, which gave them a small but certain interest, two or three per cent.

In 1855 the Limited Liability Act was passed. This act said that if a firm went bankrupt, the investor would only lose the actual amount he had put into the business, and would not be responsible for all the debts incurred. This act encouraged people to lend money to new enterprises. For instance, in the forties the railways were built by companies formed for that purpose. The amount of money required was so great that it would have been difficult to finance railway building in any other way. Privately owned firms began to register themselves as companies, and if they needed capital for expansion they would offer shares which the public could buy. The shareholders were the owners of the firm, the running of which was left to a board of directors, who sent out reports to all the shareholders of how the money was being spent.

Of course many small family firms remained, where the business passed from father to son, but the general trend was towards large concerns built on capital subscribed by the public.

Gladstone's second ministry   1880–5

Gladstone's second ministry could rightly be called the 'ministry of all the troubles'. At home he was beset by the problems in Ireland, which you will read about in the next chapter. Abroad he had difficulties both in Africa and the north-west frontier of India.

Egypt

The ruler of Egypt, called the Khedive, was hopelessly in debt, and even the selling of his shares in the Suez Canal to Britain did not free him from financial embarrassment. Those who had invested money in Egypt were worried lest their interest would not be paid. Britain and France therefore insisted on controlling the taxes and revenue of the country in the interest of the shareholders. This caused a rebellion in Egypt, led by Arabi Pasha, who declared that Egypt must get rid of all foreign control. When fifty Europeans were massacred in Alexandria, Gladstone, although he always shrank from war, felt bound to interfere.

Alexandria was bombarded and Arabi Pasha was defeated at the Battle of Tel-el-Kebir in 1882. A small British army of occupation was left in Egypt.

Sudan

To the south of Egypt, and misgoverned by it, lay the Sudan. A religious leader, calling himself the Mahdi, roused the people against their Egyptian oppressors. He claimed to be descended from the last of the twelve disciples of Mohammed. Soon he had a formidable army behind him, and the Egyptian forces were unable to check his progress.

The government in Cairo asked for British help. Gladstone was in a dilemma. We had accepted some responsibility for the country, and we had a small army there to keep order, but should British lives be lost to bolster up an unpopular régime? The Cabinet decided that our forces should be recalled from Khartoum (the capital of the Sudan) and a capable general had to be found to carry out the operation.

The press in England carried large headlines 'Gordon for the Sudan'. General Gordon had once been Governor-General there. He knew the country and he knew the people, and therefore he seemed a suitable candidate. He was asked to go to Khartoum and to report back to the government on the position there and on the best way of carrying out the evacuation. The choice of General Gordon for this difficult job was in one way unfortunate. He was not used to retreating, and once back in what he considered was his own special territory and amongst the people he knew and whom he had governed, he could not accept the idea that he should desert them and leave them to the mercies of the Mahdi, whose reputation for cruelty was well deserved.

It seemed clear to Gladstone that Gordon, who sent telegrams urging that more men and more arms should be given him, intended to hold Khartoum, and that he wanted not to withdraw, but to defeat the Mahdi.

The position grew perilous. The Mahdi's troops were slowly surrounding Khartoum and when the telegraph line was cut and no more messages came through there was panic in England. Gordon sent his second-in-command down the river by boat to take letters to Cairo explaining his position. The boat foundered on the rocks, the members of the party were discovered and killed by some followers of the Mahdi. They took Gordon's report to their chief, so now the Mahdi knew exactly how long Gordon could hold out.

Gladstone resisted for a long time the popular clamour to rescue General Gordon. He foresaw that it would mean terrible bloodshed if Britain undertook to smash the Mahdi. Finally he gave in to the demands of his Cabinet and ordered Sir Garnet Wolseley to equip an expedition to relieve Khartoum. Gordon, the only European left in the fort, tried desperately to keep up the morale of the men, and assured them each day that the promised help would arrive in a few hours.

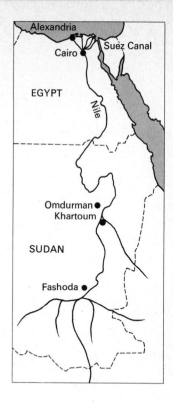

Egypt and the Sudan.

What happened during those last terrible days? We have only one account, that of a merchant, Bordeini Bey. He described how Gordon organized the defences, working with feverish energy. Food was short; numbers deserted to the Mahdi. Gordon's indifference to danger struck everyone with awe. Bordeini Bey told him that the people wanted him to cover up the windows because they offered a good mark for the enemy's bullets. Gordon brought a large lantern which held twenty-four candles. He placed it on the table in front of the window and lit the candles. Then he said:

When God was portioning out fear to all the world, at last it came to my turn and there was no fear to give me; go tell the people in Khartoum that Gordon fears nothing, for God has created him without fear.

At 3 o'clock in the morning of 26 January, 1885, the defences were breached and the Mahdi's troops rushed into the palace. According to Bordeini Bey, Gordon in his white uniform, sword in hand, stood at the top of the stairs, calm and defiant. Four Arabs rushed up to him and cried 'Oh cursed one, your hour has come.' A few seconds later Gordon was dead. His head, wrapped in a towel, was taken to the Mahdi. Two days later the relieving force arrived.

There was a furious outburst of anger in England against Gladstone. He might have defended himself by saying that Gordon had disobeyed

Reconstruction of the scene of Gordon's death published in one of the early picture magazines. Gordon is here dressed in black, which seems to contradict the report of Bordeini Bey that he was in white. Probably the artist wanted to make Gordon stand out among the white-clad Arabs.

Cavalry charge at the battle of Omdurman.

orders. He refused to do this. He also refused to carry on a war of vengeance against the Mahdi. Thirteen years later, in 1898, when Lord Salisbury was Prime Minister, the Sudan was reconquered at the Battle of Omdurman.

Fashoda

Great Britain had never made any alliances with other countries in the nineteenth century. We thought that so long as we had our navy to protect the Empire we needed no allies abroad. During the times of Palmerston and Disraeli we had thought it important to check the ambitions of Russia, a country which we thought was our most dangerous enemy. At the end of the century that idea began to look old-fashioned. Germany, a united country after 1871, had made enormous strides and was gaining in wealth and power, and was also building a navy. A triple alliance had been formed between Germany, Austria and Italy. This made France, which had been defeated by Germany in 1870, feel insecure and she made an alliance with Russia.

Great Britain then stood alone, between these two powerful blocs. Would our policy of 'splendid isolation' still be practicable? The matter was put to the test in 1898. France had possessions in North Africa, and had an ambitious plan to stretch across the continent to the Red Sea. When the French Major Marchand was leading an expedition eastwards, he hoisted the French flag at Fashoda. Great Britain objected. The statesmen of both countries hesitated. France was afraid of Germany; was it wise to be also on bad terms with Britain? Britain was beginning to see Germany as a possible rival; was it wise to be on bad terms with France? They decided to make an agreement. France promised to leave us alone in the Sudan, and Britain promised not to interfere with France's plans in Morocco.

How important this new policy was – that of friendship with France – you will understand when you read the next volume.

112

The new model craft unions

The prosperity of the country reached down to the class of skilled workers. These were the craftsmen and formed twenty per cent of the labour force. After the failure of the Grand National Consolidated Trades Union which we read about in Chapter 4, there had been a comparative lull in Trade Union activity. The most active of the workers had been in the Chartist movement. In 1851 a new kind of union was formed, the Amalgamated Society of Engineers. It was called a new model because it limited its membership to the engineers who had been apprenticed, and did not allow the others to join. It soon had a large membership. Other crafts followed this pattern, the carpenters and joiners, the bricklayers and cotton-spinners. Their policy was to avoid strikes if possible, and instead to get increases in wages by negotiation with the employers. They were unexpectedly successful. They were working in an age of expansion; the employers could afford to give rises; in fact they preferred wage rises to facing expensive strikes. These unions charged a high subscription and acted as benefit and sick clubs. The wages for these skilled workers rose to £2 a week in many industries, or even more, and as the price of food was going down, the real wages, that is what the money would buy, went up still more. The skilled worker could afford to have a house for his family, clothe them respectably, and pay for some education for his children. The Liberal Party paid the election expenses of some of them, inviting them to stand for Parliament. In return they supported the Liberal Party. They hoped to get from the Liberals the legislation they wanted. They formed what might be called the aristocracy of labour, and were very different from the gaunt and hungry workers who had fought behind the Chartist banner. It looked as if the prophecies of Gladstone would come true and soon everybody would be prosperous.

'We assist each other in time of need.' The Feltmakers' Company became one of the early benefit clubs.

WE ASSIST EACH OTHER IN TIME OF NEED.

The golden age of farming   1850–80

During these years the farmers, like the businessmen, prospered. They had feared the effects of the repeal of the Corn Laws, but in fact had found that their fears were not well founded. For one thing there was not a great deal of corn which could be brought in very cheaply, and though the price fell, it was not a catastrophic fall.

More attention was given to the science of farming. The chemistry of soil was studied and better fertilizers were used. Also there were new machines, such as the reaper and binder. This reduced the size of the labour force and so saved the farmer money.

The labourer, who had a good chance of work in the towns, was able to command a higher wage. The average in 1870 was twelve shillings a week. This did not compare favourably with the wages in the town, but it was an improvement on the starvation wages of the earlier part of the century.

The end of the golden age

The year 1878 was a very wet one and the harvest was bad. The following year also had a bad harvest. The farmers hoped that they had had a merely temporary setback. But changes on the other side of the Atlantic were changing the position of the British farmer. Railways in America and Canada had been built across the prairies and corn from these virgin lands could be brought over to Britain and sold for a much lower price than the English farmer was obliged to charge. In ten years the price dropped from 45s. a quarter to 31s. It no longer paid the farmer to grow corn. Refrigeration on ships meant that frozen meat could be sent from the Argentine, Australia, and New Zealand and sold for half the price of the English meat. Many of the farmers faced ruin and bankruptcy.

Soup kitchen for distressed people in London's East End.

Farmers turned to producing milk, because milk was the one commodity which had to be produced in this country. They also went in for more market gardening. The prosperous people in the towns could afford to buy wholesome fresh foods. But even with this policy of dairy farming and vegetable-growing, at the end of the nineteenth century farming was the Cinderella of occupations in England.

The other side of the picture in the towns

Foreign visitors coming to England were all struck by the contrast between the great riches and the great poverty. One of the marvels of London was to be seen every day in Hyde Park, when the aristocratic ladies drove in their luxurious carriages attended by liveried footmen. It was a parade of elegance and refinement. At the other end of London, for miles down the East End, there was a mass of overcrowding and misery. While the skilled workers were improving their position, the unskilled were unorganized and relied on chance for work. There was no unemployment pay. Much work, such as building, was seasonal; when the labourers could not work because of the weather, they had

Dinner in the West End.

114

Bluegate Fields, a slum street in London, 1872.

nothing to fall back on. Trade varied, it moved up and down. If there was even a slight trade depression, thousands would be out of work.

A retired Liverpool ship-owner, Charles Booth, made a careful survey of certain parts of London and published his results in a book called *The Life and Labour of the People of London*. He estimated that one-third of the population was destitute. A later survey of the city of York revealed the same proportion, and showed that it was not only London which had its underlayer of poverty. Dr Barnardo startled people by telling them how thousands of children had no homes, how they slept under archways, with no parental care, how they were just thrown on the city to pick up a living as they could. Several middle-class people took up the question of the way this section of the poor lived. One of them, Beatrice Potter, afterwards famous as Mrs Sidney Webb, worked herself in a small clothing factory to find out about conditions of work. It was discovered that a great deal of work was done by women in their own homes and was called piece-work. For instance, a woman at this time sewed on the buttons and made the buttonholes of a dozen shirts for threepence, providing her own thread and buttons. It seemed the same as the time when Hood had written his *Song of the Shirt* with the lines:

Sewing at once with a double thread
A shroud as well as a shirt.

'Needle money.' Piece-workers like this one were grossly underpaid by the clothing manufacturers who employed them.

What was the solution of this problem which seemed to disprove the happy idea of the Liberals that soon everyone would be well off? Private charity might do something, but it was only a drop in the ocean.

'The docker's tanner'   1889

Down in London's East End, the docks stretched for miles, and the roughest and poorest of the workers were the dockers. Private companies owned the docks and they contracted with gangers to supply the men to load and unload the ships. Some of the men were regulars, called the 'royals', but most of them were casuals. When a ship docked the men went to the sheds where the gangers gave out the work, and fought each other like wild beasts to get hold of a ticket which allowed them to work a two-hour shift for fivepence an hour. Four times a day the men were taken on. Sometimes the gangers threw rubber rings at the crowd of struggling men, and the ones who caught the rings got the tickets. If a man were lucky he might get work for three or four days a week, if he were unlucky he might be idle for days. And it was hard work, for which men needed to be fit.

Tillett, Mann and Crook were three men who had all had experience in organizing men in a union, though none of them were dockers. They told the dockers that they must get organized. They explained the need to stick together. They knew it was the only way they would improve conditions. Day after day they talked at the dock gates, urging the men not to fight each other, but to fight the dock companies instead. Then one day a good chance seemed to come. There was a dispute over the unloading of a ship called the *Lady Armstrong*. The men claimed they were being cheated out of their bonus. Ben Tillett rushed down to the docks and harangued the men, told them they must come out on strike if they wanted results, and they must all come out together. They agreed to come out and to demand sixpence an hour. This claim became known as 'the docker's tanner'. The strike was on, and Ben Tillett knew he had taken on the hardest job of his life.

The dock companies were not much alarmed. 'Give them a few weeks and hunger will bring the men back.' The men's leaders knew this only too well. Somehow they would have to feed 4,000 men and their families. There were no union funds. If they succeeded, it could only be by a miracle. The first thing to do was to see that all the docks, right down the Thames to Tilbury, came out. Speakers were hastily sent out to explain the position and a series of pickets organized to keep out the blacklegs, who would certainly be brought in if the strike lasted more than a few days. Another problem was how to keep the men disciplined, men who had never before been organized. Ben Tillett collected crowds of them every morning to march into the City and to Hyde Park. For one thing it gave the men heart. As they marched they carried collecting boxes, and they showed the City and the West End that they were there. The newspapers could not ignore them. John Burns, a well-known personality in the City, joined the movement. Londoners were amazed when they saw the marchers; these respectable, orderly marchers were the wild men, whose disorderliness was a legend. Some of the papers started subscriptions; money poured in from the most unexpected sources. But even with the money which was sent, the organizers had a nerve-racking time. The men could not hold out for ever on the little money the strike committee could give them.

A doll representing a docker's child, carried on the dockers' march.

They soon had other help. All down the Thames, from the Isle of Dogs to Tilbury, the river was blocked with ships which were waiting to unload their cargoes, and the shipping companies sympathized with the dockers and urged the directors of the docks to give way. Nearly all the newspapers also expressed sympathy with the dockers. Churchmen took up their cause; Cardinal Archbishop Manning, the Bishop of London and one or two other men, including the Lord Mayor of London, formed a conciliation committee. They got the directors to agree to the 'tanner', but not until the New Year. Ben Tillett went down on Monday morning to Tower Hill where the dockers met, and told them the terms of the offer. Would they hold out longer and get what they wanted now? The winter was coming; they would need the money when the cold weather started. They voted to stay out. Notices began to appear scrawled on the houses 'No rent till the docker gets his tanner', and this song was sung on the marches:

'Father Neptune' carried by
the dockers in their procession.

Sing a song of sixpence,
Dockers on the strike.
Guinea pigs as hungry,
As the greedy pike.
Till the docks are opened,
Burns for you will speak.
Courage lads, and you'll win,
Well within the week.

After that Monday meeting Ben Tillett went into the office where
the meal tickets were given out, wondering how they were going to get
through the week. Then the miracle happened. Like manna dropped
from Heaven, money came pouring in from Australia. The papers
there had carried the news of the strike, and a wave of sympathy swept
through the country. The Mayor of Brisbane held a meeting and urged
every town to do the same. The government said money could be cabled

free; the banks made no charges. Profits from sports events were contributed; in all a country of less than 4,000,000 inhabitants sent £30,000. It saved the strike. The leaders said afterwards that but for this money, the men could not have held out. Cardinal Manning, who had been disappointed that the men had not accepted the earlier offer, intervened once more. The dock companies gave in. The dockers had won their tanner. Not a very big advance you may say, only a penny an hour extra. Actually it meant much more than that. A trade union was formed. It had been shown that the least privileged of the workers could organize and achieve solid results. This union was different from the other craft unions; it was a big industrial union of all the workers in one industry. Later it merged into a bigger one, called the Transport and General Workers' Union.

The Finance Committee of the Dock Strike issuing meal tickets at a pub in Poplar, London, which was the strikers' headquarters. (John Burns is third from the right.)

The Independent Labour Party

There were groups of people at this time who were disturbed by the conditions which had been so dramatically revealed. They argued that there was something fundamentally wrong with the way the industrial life of Britain was organized. Workers had no real security. If there was a slump, through no fault of their own, they became unemployed. And in any case their employment was in the hands of the owners of big business, the capitalists as they were called. They had the profits from manufacture, but had the workers no right to some of the profits too?

The workers, by their labour, had made the capital. These people called themselves socialists; they said that neither the Liberals nor the Conservatives could cure the ills of society, they could only patch up things here and there. What was wanted was a system in which individual men did not own the factories and machines.

Keir Hardie was one of the first Socialist leaders in this country. He was a Scottish miner who had started work at the age of ten. His family had a long tradition of trade union work; one of his ancestors, Andrew Hardie, had been hanged in Bonniemuir in 1820, after a strike. He said that a new party was needed, a party of workers, not just a few trade unionists who hung on to the coat tails of the Liberals. In 1893 a small group of like-minded men founded the Independent Labour Party, and put up five candidates in the election. Keir Hardie in the House of Commons was something the members had never experienced before. They were used to violent debates where the two parties had attacked each other with vigour. But these arguments had been couched in educated language. Keir Hardie broke in with brutal frankness and told the House of Commons to turn their attention to the 1,300,000 unemployed. In the year 1894 there was a terrible mining disaster, in which 260 miners were killed. The following day the President of the French Republic was assassinated. Parliament sent a message of condolence to France, but did not think it was necessary to send one to Cilnydd in Wales; it was enough, said the government spokesman,

Keir Hardie in his later years addressing a crowd in Trafalgar Square.

if they just expressed their sympathy in the House of Commons. Keir Hardie was so enraged that when a baby (afterwards Edward VIII) was born to the Duchess of York he voted against a message of congratulations. The House of Commons had been used to quiet and respectful trade union leaders. This was something new.

The Labour Party   1900

The Independent Labour Party remained a small group and made little headway. Keir Hardie realized that it must have the backing of the trade unions before it could be really effective. This was debated at the Trades Union Congress and it was finally decided to form a Parliamentary Representation Society, which should work to get its own members elected to Parliament. There was at first a good deal of doubt about the wisdom of this policy. An event in 1900 hastened the decision of the unions. There was a strike on a little railway in Wales, the Taff Vale Railway. At the end of it the railway directors sued the trade union for the losses they had had to bear during the strike. The court upheld the directors and the union had to pay out a large sum. This decision angered the trade unions. If that was the law then they must get into Parliament and alter it. The Labour Party was born in 1900, partly as a result of the Taff Vale decision. It is important to notice that it was not a socialist party. Very few of its members sympathized with Keir Hardie's ideas. It was a trade union party formed to fight for the rights of trade unions. The old tradition of two parties opposing each other, Roundheads and Cavaliers, Whigs and Tories, Liberals and Conservatives was broken. A third party had entered the lists.

Dates to remember

1867   Second Reform Act
1872   Secret Ballot Act
1875   Plimsoll Line
        Climbing Boys Act
        Purchase of Suez Canal shares
1889   Dock strike
1900   Foundation of the Labour Party

Things to do

1   Find out whether a Conservative or a Liberal represented your town during the years 1867–1900.
2   Many people opposed the Secret Ballot Act because they said people should have the courage of their opinions and not be afraid to own up to them. Do you think this was a sensible objection?
3   Discuss whether examinations are the best way of making appointments to positions.
4   Find out whether there is a Trades Council in your town and how many trade union branches belong to it.

A London sweep.

Interesting people to read about: Dr Barnardo, Mrs Sidney Webb, Keir Hardie.

Books to read

Alan Moorehead, *The White Nile*, Penguin
G. Pattison, *Outline of Trade Union History*, Barrie & Rockliffe
A. Stafford, *A Match to Fire the Thames*, Hodder & Stoughton
N. Wymer, *Dr Barnardo*, Longmans

1. Oh, every eve-ning af- ter dark The blackleg miners
3. They'll take your tools and clothes as well And throw them into the

creep to work, With cor-du-roys and coal- y shirt, The dir-ty black-leg min-ers.
pit of hell. It's down you go and fare you well, You dir-ty black-leg min-ers.

2. They take their picks and down they go To dig the coal that
4. So join the u-nion while you may, Don't wait un- til your

lies below, And there isn't a woman in all the town Would
dy-ing day, For that may not be far away, You

Repeat   Last time

look at a blackleg miner.
dirty blackleg miner.

Chapter 8
Ireland

The wearing of the green

Oh Paddy dear, and did you hear
    The news that's going round?
The shamrock is forbid by law
    To grow on Irish ground.
St Patrick's day no more we'll keep,
    His colours can't be seen.
For there's a cruel law against
    The wearing of the green.

I met with Napper Tandy,
    And he took me by the hand.
Says he, 'How's poor old Ireland,
    And how does she stand?'
She's the most distressful country,
    That ever yet was seen.
They're hanging men and women there,
    For wearing of the green.

A shamrock, emblem of Ireland.

Why there was a problem of Ireland

When Gladstone heard the news that his party had won the election of 1868 and that he would therefore become Prime Minister, he was in the garden of his home in Cheshire, chopping down a tree. He laid down the axe and said, 'My mission is to pacify Ireland.' Do you wonder why he should have said Ireland, and made no mention of Scotland or Wales? All these countries together formed the United Kingdom of Great Britain. Why then was Ireland different?

To understand why that country should be uppermost in Gladstone's mind, we have to understand what had happened before he became Prime Minister. The Irish people were Celts who originally spoke Gaelic. Over the centuries, ever since the reign of Henry II, the English had tried to gain control of the country and had set up their government in the city of Dublin. The Irish had remained Catholics when both the English and the Scots had turned to Protestantism. This meant that the enemies of England, first Spain, then France (both Roman Catholic countries), tried to get help from Ireland against England. The English government were aware of this danger, and so they tried to colonize Ireland; they took the estates away from the native Irish lords and gave them to English settlers. James I handed over a large part of Ulster, in the north of Ireland, to Scottish farmers, so that this one area of

Ireland became largely Protestant. Cromwell defeated the Irish who had supported Charles I and gave land there to his soldiers; William III had to conquer Ireland before he felt his throne secure, and after the Battle of the Boyne he handed out estates to his generals. In this way much of the land of Ireland passed from its original owners and belonged to the Protestant English. The Whig government of William III's reign was so afraid that the Irish would support the exiled Stuarts that they passed laws, called the Penal Laws, which were designed to keep the Catholics down.

Under these laws no Catholic could have any post in the government or teach in a school, or own a horse worth more than £5. Priests had to be registered. If a member of a Catholic family became a Protestant, he must inherit all the family's property. The Catholic tenants had to pay land taxes (called tithes) to the Church of Ireland, which was a Protestant Church, even though they did not belong to it. The English, too,

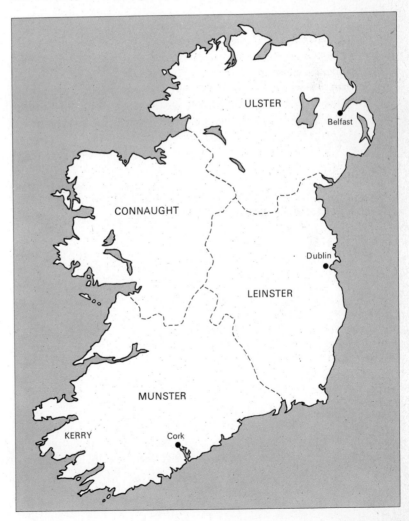

Map of Ireland.

The home of the English Viceroy in Phoenix Park, Dublin.

were jealous of Irish trade. They forbade the Irish to export woollen cloth, or cattle, butter and cheese. With their trade ruined and their religion persecuted there seemed little chance that the Irish Catholics would be dangerous to England.

There was a Parliament in Dublin, but of course only Protestants could vote for the members, and every act passed had to be approved by the English Parliament. This was resented by many of the Protestant middle-class, who suffered from the laws which regulated Irish trade. They seized the chance, when England was fighting the American colonies, to declare that their Parliament was independent. This was in 1782, and eleven years later the Irish Parliament gave Catholics the right to vote, though they still could not sit in Parliament.

Like all the other countries in Europe, Ireland was influenced by the ideas of the French Revolution. A young Protestant lawyer from Ulster, called Wolfe Tone, formed the society of the United Irishmen, which Protestants and Catholics joined. He boldly declared for an independent Irish Republic, and went to France to ask for help. The United Irishmen roused the patriotic feelings of the Irish. Pitt was alarmed at the success of this society and at the influence of Wolfe Tone. He sent spies into the movement, with the result that the names of the leaders and the plans for a rebellion were well known to the English government. Storms round the south coast of Ireland prevented the French from landing, and in 1798 the Irish rebelled without the hoped-for help from France. They were defeated by the English troops.

The two leaders, Wolfe Tone and Lord Edward Fitzgerald, were taken prisoner. Wolfe Tone was said to have committed suicide in prison. Lord Edward lingered several days and finally died from his wounds. The memory of these men, 'the men of 98', was kept alive in Ireland. They were the first martyrs for Irish independence. Their bravery and the cruelty with which the rebellion was crushed made a lasting impression on the Irish people.

126

The Act of Union and the famine

Pitt had long decided that the only way to overcome what he thought of as the Irish danger was to join the Irish to the English Parliament, as had been done a hundred years before with the English and Scottish Parliaments. To do this involved heavy bribes to members of the Dublin Parliament. In addition he promised that a bill would be passed to give the Catholics equal rights with the Protestants. In 1800 the Act of Union was passed in both Parliaments and after this the Irish members sat in Westminster. But when George III was faced with signing the bill giving the Catholics their freedom, he refused his signature and the bill was dropped. Catholic emancipation was finally granted in 1829 in order to avoid another revolt in Ireland. The Irish leader, O'Connell, began a campaign to get the Act of Union repealed.

The act which gave the Catholics equal rights with Protestants was a measure of justice but it did not make Ireland prosperous. The trouble was that the people were too poor. The peasant holdings were small, too small often to support a family properly, and as the population increased, these holdings were divided up into even smaller units. The English peasants, when they had been driven off the land, had gone into the towns to work in the factories. Ireland had no factories; in Ireland a man had either to have a piece of land or starve. They grew little corn; what they did grow and any animals they reared went to pay rent to the landlords and tithes to the Church. For themselves they grew

Inside a mud cabin at Kildare.

potatoes. From a given piece of land more food can be produced from growing potatoes than from corn. Thus the Irish, with such very small holdings, relied on this one form of food. The danger of this system is that if anything happens to the crop the people have nothing else to fall back on. In 1845 a potato blight attacked the crop in many parts of the country and there was great distress. This had often happened before and the tradition was that after a bad year the crop the following year would be exceptionally good. In 1846 the potato crop promised well, then suddenly in the space of a fortnight all over the country it was totally destroyed by blight. The Irish had no food for the winter. It was not a partial failure. It was total and meant starvation. Appeals were made to the government, but in vain. People in England argued that the stories must be exaggerated; it could not possibly be as bad as some of the Irish were saying. We can perhaps imagine what it is like to be short of food. It is difficult to think what it must be like to be completely without food.

A report sent to the Duke of Wellington from an Irish J.P. said:

I was surprised to find the wretched hamlet apparently deserted. I entered some of the hovels to ascertain the cause, and the scenes which presented themselves were such as no tongue or pen can convey the slightest idea of. In the first, six famished and ghastly skeletons, to all appearances dead, were huddled in a corner on some filthy straw, their sole covering what seemed a ragged horsecloth, and their wretched legs hanging out, naked below the knees. I approached in horror and found by a low moaning they were alive, they were in a fever, four children, a woman and what had once been a man.

Scenes such as these were common, and reports came of famished people dying by the roadside.

Peel repealed the Corn Laws and large quantities of maize meal were sent in. But what the politicians in Westminster could not understand was that the Irish had no money even for the cheapest sort of food. The

A funeral at Skibbereen in Cork during the famine.

Soup kitchen run by Quakers at Cork, 1847.

desperateness of the situation was only understood later. Then the government started relief and men were paid for working on roads and digging ditches. The conditions would have been even worse if private charity had not helped. Thousands of pounds were raised in England and food centres were set up. Finally the government too did this, but as it limited its help to those who had a farm no larger than a quarter of an acre, many starving men abandoned their lands to get food. All this time boats loaded with cattle, butter and cheese were leaving the Irish ports. The government were urged to close the ports and distribute the food in the country, but said that they could not do this because it would interfere with normal trade.

It is reckoned that one million people in Ireland died of starvation and disease, a quarter of a million managed to get to England, and a million went to America, transported in crowded and insanitary ships. Those exiles carried with them bitter memories and nursed a hatred

The village of Moveen in 1849, deserted and in ruins as a result of the potato famine.

against England which had let them starve, while boats left the country full of food produced in Ireland.

The Fenians and Gladstone

Some of the Irish in America never forgot the land of their origin. They formed a society called 'The Irish Republican Brotherhood', or 'Fenians' as it was also called. They collected money to buy arms to send to Ireland and soon there were branches on both sides of the Atlantic. As in the past information was given to the government by spies, and the Fenian rising planned for 1867 never took place. The leaders were arrested before the outbreak occurred. The arrested men were brought to England. A group of Fenians tried to blow up Clerkenwell prison where the men were held, and another group fired on a van which was carrying some of the Fenians to jail in Manchester. They did not succeed in rescuing the prisoners, but they killed a policeman, and people felt that the Irish struggle was being brought over to England.

Gladstone's policy

This was the situation when Gladstone became Prime Minister in 1868. No wonder that he exclaimed that his mission was to pacify Ireland. Gladstone had a sincere sympathy for any people who were trying to get freedom. He knew Ireland had suffered from its connexion with England and he wanted to right the wrongs of that unhappy country.

He was a strong supporter of the Anglican Church. This did not, however, blind him to the fact that it was unjust to make Irish Catholics support a church to which they did not belong; therefore in 1869 he passed an act to disestablish the Church of England in Ireland. This meant that in future it must support itself.

He was next concerned about the land. As we have explained the land was the only way by which the Irishmen could live, except in Ulster where there was a linen industry. There was no system of long leases, as there was in England; a peasant rented his land for only one year at a time. If he improved it in any way the landlord could increase the rent. If the first man could not pay the higher rent, there were plenty of others eager to get a farm, who would pay it, or anyway offer to pay it. Gladstone passed his first Land Act which stated that a landlord could not increase the rent because of any improvements the tenant might have made, and that if a tenant left he was entitled to compensation for any improvements.

The Land League

For six years, from 1874 until 1880, Disraeli was Prime Minister and Gladstone was not able to introduce any more bills about Ireland. The situation there did not improve; in fact disturbances broke out in the west. The Land Act was not as successful as Gladstone had hoped it would be; the landlords and tenants found it easy to make private agree-

Captain Boycott was obliged to bring in his own harvest with the help of his family, since no labourers would **work for him. He was** protected by soldiers.

ments and so avoid the terms of the act. A Land League was formed by Michael Davitt. He urged all the farmers not to pay rents any higher than what was fixed by the League. The movement spread like wildfire. Agents dared not go out to collect rents. The blowing of a horn was the signal that a bailiff or policeman was on the way. The peasants would drive their animals out into the bog, so that they could not be taken instead of rent. Landlords went round in twos and threes, armed. If a barn was burned, or other injuries done to a landlord's property, no Irish jury would convict. No man dared accept a farm at a high rent. If he did he was shunned. No shop would serve him, no one would work for him. He was just left alone. The first man to receive this treatment was Captain Boycott, and so we get the verb, to boycott.

A new leader had appeared in Parliament, Charles Stewart Parnell. He realized that the small Irish party in the House of Commons could be very effective if the members made themselves a nuisance. He disciplined the party very well, and carried out his policy of obstruction. Whatever the subject under discussion, someone or other of the Irish members would get up and talk about Ireland. Parnell would appear in the House of Commons, and pass a note to one of his supporters: 'Talk for half an hour on Irish butter' or 'Talk for three-quarters of an hour on the Cork railway.' This forced attention on Ireland, because it delayed the business of the House.

Gladstone's policy – Home Rule

In 1880 Gladstone became Prime Minister again in this disturbed situation. He made a valiant effort to settle the vexed question of the land,

Parnell leads out nineteen of his followers, expelled from the House of Commons in 1881 for disregarding the Speaker's authority.

and brought in a second Land Act, the three F's; these were fair rent, to be fixed by the government, fixity of tenure, which meant that no tenant could be evicted except for non-payment of rent, and free sale, the tenants could dispose of their leases if they wished. But this act did not bring peace. The Land League said the government valued the farms too high; the rick-burning and violence continued. All this brought Gladstone to the conviction that only self-government would bring peace to Ireland. He brought in a Home Rule Bill, which was defeated in the House of Lords. Later he brought in a second one, which was also thrown out by the Lords. This question of Home Rule for Ireland split the Liberal party: half of them would not follow Gladstone and called themselves 'Liberal Unionists', because they believed in the union of Ireland with England. Later they joined the Conservative Party and that is why it is sometimes called the Unionist Party. You still see the words 'Unionist Club' outside Conservative clubs, though the words now have no meaning.

The Conservative policy in Ireland

The Conservatives appointed Balfour as Secretary for Ireland. He had a tough policy. The magistrates were given military support so that they would not be afraid to convict. Balfour was determined that what were called the 'outrages' must stop. The Royal Irish Constabulary was strengthened.

132

Balfour's land policy was to buy up the land from such landowners as wanted to get rid of their troubled estates, and sell the farms to the tenants, the payment to extend over forty years. Many landowners accepted this with relief. They had had twenty years of uncertainty and disorder, so they thankfully took their money. In this way the question of the relation of landlord to peasant farmer was solved by the peasant farmer becoming the owner of his land.

The Irish renaissance

A great change had come over the middle-classes in Ireland. In the eighteenth century there had been so little opportunity for anyone with ambitions to prosper in such an impoverished country, that many Irishmen had gone to England. Goldsmith and Sheridan and Burke are all examples of this. Now that Ireland was governed by the same laws as England, there was no longer any restriction on trade; the middle-classes began to prosper. They stayed in Ireland. They grew interested in their country and proud of its past.

Scholars began to investigate the early history of the country. They studied the old monuments, the Round Towers, the ruins of the monasteries. Legends were revived, the Celtic stories of Cuchullain and Deirdre. They remembered Brian Boru, the High King of Ireland who had defeated the Danes at the Battle of Clontarf in 1014. And more than anything, the scholars began to mourn the fact that the old language, Gaelic, was dying out, and was only spoken by the peasants in the west. Great efforts were made to revive Gaelic. Classes were organized in all the towns, all patriotic young Irish people were exhorted to learn 'their own language'. Learned professors rushed down to Kerry where they could hear the language spoken every day by the folk in the countryside. Unfortunately the only literature there was in Gaelic was old, as far from modern Irish as Chaucer is from modern English. The peasants had kept alive their folktales, their songs and dances. These were eagerly seized on by students and written down. Early in the century

A poem written in Gaelic. Caitlin Ni Uallachain is a girl's name.

Caitlín ní Uallacáin

Ó meaṛaimiḋ naċ calm ḟinn ḋen ḃuaiṗt ṛan Spáinn
Aċt meallaḋ ṛuiġe ċum caṫa claiḋim ḋo ṫaḃaiṗt i ḋtṛáṫ;
Ḃeiḋ Ġalla aṛíṛ ḋ'á leaġaḋ linn le lúṫ áṛ láṁ,
Aġuṛ mac an ṛíoġ aġ Caitlín Ní Uallacáin.

We may think it a fine thing to seek refuge from our sorrow in Spain,
but it is sweeter to stay and do battle with the sword;
we shall defeat the foe by our strength,
and the king's son shall have Caitlin Ni Uallachain.

133

the Irish middle-class had looked down on the peasants for speaking this strange tongue. Now they all wanted to learn it.

Irish writers stayed in Ireland and Irish playwrights had their plays produced on an Irish stage. The Abbey Theatre in Dublin had a world-wide renown. Although the country was still joined to England and Irish members had to sit in the Parliament at Westminster, the Irish themselves were turning their backs on England and becoming a separate nation.

Dates to remember

1798	Rebellion of the United Irishmen under Wolfe Tone
1800	Union of the two Parliaments of Westminster and Dublin
1845–6	Irish Famine
1870	Gladstone's First Land Act
1881	Gladstone's Second Land Act
1886	First Home Rule Bill
1891	Land Purchase Act

Things to do

1 Make a list of all the writers you can find who came from Ireland. Then find and read examples of their work.

Far left: William Butler Yeats, Irish poet and dramatist.
Left: George Bernard Shaw, Irish playwright.

2 Find the meanings of the words 'stirabout', 'shillelagh', 'jaunting car'.
3 What other parts of the British Isles other than Ireland speak a Celtic language?
4 Who are the Orangemen and what day do they celebrate?
5 Find out about the lives of Wolfe Tone, Parnell, Lady Gregory.

Books to read

Maria Edgeworth, *Castle Rackrent*, Oxford University Press
George Moore, *The Untilled Field*, Heinemann

Oh - Paddy dear, and did you hear the news that's go-ing round The
shamrock is for-bid by law to grow on I-rish ground. St
Patrick's day no more we'll keep, his colours can't be seen. For
there's a cruel law a-gainst the wearing of the green.

Chapter 9
Town and village life

The drift into the towns

In the year 1800 10 per cent of the population worked in towns and the rest in the country. At the end of the century the position was nearly reversed. Only 25 per cent worked in the country, 75 per cent in the towns. The population in 1800 was 9,000,000, in 1900 it was 37,000,000. If we look at these figures we see what an enormous change took place in a hundred years; not only were there three times as many people at the end of the century as there were at the beginning, but nearly all of them were concentrated in the towns. We can also see some of the problems which would arise. Where would all these people live when they streamed into the towns to work in factories?

Nowadays when a new town or a suburb is built it is carefully planned, but in 1800 and for many years afterwards there were no rules or regulations about how houses should be built. Anyone, provided that he bought the land, could build how he liked. A man setting up a factory would build it as near a coalmine as possible, then hastily

Birmingham in 1848.

put up houses for the workers he would need. Anyone setting out to make a fortune in manufacture would not want to waste money on providing comfortable and airy houses. He put up as many as possible on the land and crowded the workers in them. They had to live near the factory, so they rented a room or a cellar in a jerry-built house for themselves and their families, because there was no other choice.

What the new towns were like

After all, the employer might argue, they were used to nothing better in the villages they came from, where overcrowding was the rule. There, however, the people had outside their homes plenty of fresh air unpolluted by smoke from the mills. Their children could play in the fields or walk in the woods. Even if the cottages were small and stuffy, the villagers spent most of their time working in a healthy atmosphere. Nearly all the towns in the eighteenth century were what we should now call villages, so that these industrial towns which sprang up in Lancashire, Yorkshire and the Midlands were something new in English life. Conditions which, if not ideal, were at least bearable in a small community, became terrible when thousands of people were huddled together.

Sheffield in 1858, spreading up over the hills in the background.

When a town is built now the first things to be supplied are water and a drainage system. In the first part of the nineteenth century neither of these necessities was attended to. In the villages water had

been drawn from wells, and a cesspit or an earth closet had been used for sanitation. Doubtless the water in the villages was sometimes contaminated, but the danger was a hundred times worse in the new towns where the well and the cesspit were never far apart. Not every house had its own pump. Often there would be one at the end of a row of houses from which all the people had to draw their water. Rubbish was quite simply thrown into the streets. It is difficult for us now to imagine the filth and the squalor which arose. Many of the houses were built 'back to back', which means that there was only one door leading to the street and the walls of the rooms at the back were the back of another house facing a different street. The houses had no backyards and that is why all refuse was thrown into the road.

We have descriptions of these towns, mostly given by doctors who could not avoid going into the overcrowded slums. In Liverpool one doctor writes of a street called Freemason's Row:

Victorian housing. The yards contain outside toilets.

138

A court of houses, the floors of which were below the public street, and the area of the whole court was a floating mass of putrefying vegetable and animal matter so dreadfully offensive that I was obliged to beat a hasty retreat. Yet the whole of the houses were inhabited.

Stories like this could be repeated about every big provincial town. London had its own special problems. Although it was not an industrial town, yet it grew very rapidly. The middle-classes left the centre of the town for the inner suburbs, and their old houses were let out in single rooms to families, so that what were once pleasant and prosperous streets became as wretched as the new slums in Lancashire. Lord Shaftesbury described Frying Pan Alley in Holborn:

In the first house that I turned into there was a single room: the window was very small and the light came in through the door. The young woman there said 'Look there at that great hole; the landlord will not mend it. I have every night to sit and watch, or my husband sits up to watch, because that hole is over a common sewer and the rats come up, twenty at a time, and if we did not watch for them they would eat the baby up.'

London had several small streams, for example the River Fleet, which ran into the Thames, and all the sewage flowed along these channels into the Thames. Some of the drinking water sold to people came from this same river.

Why should so many people leave the country to settle in a town where they would be worse housed than cattle? One reason was the lure of higher wages. In the country the wage at the beginning of the century was 7s. or 8s. a week; in the town a man could get 15s. or even more. Then, too, there was no prospect of anything better in the country; there was no chance of getting and owning a little land, whereas in the town a man with luck might improve his position and even get rich. Bad conditions are easier to bear if there is a hope of

People queueing for water in Frying Pan Alley. The pipe *(right)* provided the water-supply for many houses and the water was turned on for only twenty minutes a day.

something better. New factories were being built all the time; things were changing rapidly. In the country life was stagnant.

The improvement of the towns

Why then did people not complain of the foul smells and the general squalor? Middle-class people avoided the slums of the towns; they had no need to go into the crowded courts. The regular visitors, doctors and clergymen, did try to draw attention to the degrading conditions. Dickens thundered about them. But the difficulty was that it was nobody's business to do anything. There was no man who had the authority to order a manure heap to be removed from the middle of the road, or to insist that water should be supplied to a house.

Men were woken up to the dangers of allowing these insanitary conditions by an outbreak of cholera in 1831. Disease knows no frontiers and it travelled to the rich quarters of the towns. The fear of cholera made the government listen to the protests of the radicals who had for a long time pointed out the horrors of what was happening to the children brought up in these wretched hovels. In 1835 the Whig government passed an act called the Municipal Corporations Act which allowed the town councils to raise rates from householders and use the money for cleaning the town. Hitherto the only rate had been the Poor Rate. This act was the beginning of the general improvement of the towns.

Even when an enthusiastic town council wanted to supply proper drainage and water, it often faced difficulties of engineering. At first the plumbers did not understand how to make the joints in the pipes, and so the sewage would seep up into the street. In 1847 there was another epidemic of cholera, and this made the government realize that more action was needed. Chadwick, who had made himself so unpopular over the New Poor Law, pushed hard for improvements. In 1848 the Public Health Act was passed. By this a board was set up with wide powers; it could force a town or district to set up a local Board of Health.

In 1875 another act was passed, appointing Medical Officers of Health for every town and district. These officers had wide powers; for instance they could build fever hospitals. Sanitary inspectors were also appointed and these dealt with water supply and drainage. They could insist on public baths and wash-houses. They inspected slaughterhouses and markets where food was sold. All these measures made the towns cleaner, healthier and pleasanter. By the end of the century, though the working-class parts of the towns might be overcrowded, at least the first necessities of health were provided for.

Middle-class houses

If you look at the picture on the opposite page you will see the kind of house which was built in the middle of the nineteenth century. Notice that it is irregular in shape, there are different roof levels and a lot of decoration all over the front of the house. We noticed in Chapter 7 how

A house built for a rich
Victorian family.

there was at this time a tremendous boom in trade and this created a
class of wealthy people. Everyone is proud of having achieved something
and these businessmen were proud of having made so much money and
wanted to display it. They moved away from their factories into the
suburbs and had expensive houses built for them. They thought that the
more variety in design and the more decoration there was, the grander
the house would be. They could show the world what important people
they were.

There was a fashion at this time to admire everything which was
made in the Middle Ages. Sir Walter Scott's novels were popular, and
people thought that the Gothic style of building, the style of our
churches, was the most beautiful in the world. Men began to imitate
this style when they built houses. What is suitable for a church or a
castle is not necessarily suitable for a dwelling-place and when the
architects tried to adapt this style, the result was often a house designed
with an odd mixture of gables, turrets and battlements, everything in
fact which people thought romantic. It was not a very practical way to
design a house. For instance, the purpose of a window is to let in light,
and if it is placed flat in the wall the maximum amount of light will
shine into the room. But the Victorian architects liked long narrow
windows and often they jutted out from the wall, which meant that the
rooms inside would be dark. Imitations were sometimes carried to
absurd lengths. A house might be provided with a minstrels' gallery, as

St Pancras Station.

in a medieval baronial hall, though in the nineteenth century there were no minstrels. If you go into one of our beautiful old cathedrals, you may see some windows of stained glass. They look like jewels against the grey stone. There was a fashion of putting bits of crude coloured glass in the windows in the hall or on the landing. The effect of this was quite different from the effect of the stained glass in the churches.

The Prince Consort planned a house for the royal family on Deeside and chose as his model an old Scottish castle. These castles had small windows, built with an eye to defence. The Prince had no need to fear that he would be attacked by Highland marauders, yet he put in narrow slit windows and turrets.

It is impossible to write about a style of mid-Victorian architecture. There were several styles, all of them imitations of what had been built in the past.

Public buildings shared the same fate. One example is St Pancras Station in London. The front of the station is a riot of Gothic decoration. How extraordinary to make a station look like a red brick cathedral.

What the very rich people do sets the fashion for those who have less money. All the small houses were designed with the same idea of plenty of decoration. Rows and rows of houses were built with gables. In fact the English builder could hardly think of a house unless it had a gable. Yet they are unpractical, the cause of many leaking roofs and serve no purpose whatsoever.

Right: A Fleet Street traffic jam before the days of the motor-car: open buses, brewers' drays and sheep. (St Paul's Cathedral is in the background.)

Above: Buses were run by private companies who competed for passengers. In this *Punch* cartoon of 1882 the fat lady and her child are being 'persuaded' by two rival bus-conductors to use their transport.

Left: Boy crossing-sweepers.

The streets

The streets not only looked but sounded different from the present time. Instead of the noise of the motor-car you heard the clip-clop of the horses. Carriages, carts and riders jostled together. There were often sideshows in the streets. Punch and Judy shows were the most common. Children would crowd round to watch the drama of Punch and his wife. In the winter afternoons the muffin man would come along, ringing his bell. On his head he carried a tray covered with a baize cloth, under which lay the muffins. People ran out to buy his wares. As the roads were dirty, ladies had to gather their skirts into one hand when they crossed the street. The obliging crossing-sweeper ran in front to brush the dirt away, and was rewarded with a penny. One sight is happily no longer there, the dancing bear. These wretched-looking creatures would be led round the streets on a chain, and would be made to perform some miserable steps to amuse the passers-by. The most cheerful sounds were those of the barrel organs, played by Italians. There was always a monkey with the organ-grinder, dressed up in a red coat. These men did a good trade. They were either rewarded for their music or else given money to go into the next street. A foreign writer who thought that the English towns were gloomy places said that the one gay and happy sight in the London streets was to see the children dancing round a barrel organ.

Below: Dancing round a barrel organ.

Pictures

The Victorians liked plenty of pictures in their houses. They would have rejected a plain wall as ugly; in fact they often hung so many pictures on the walls that the wallpaper, itself highly patterned, could scarcely be seen.

They favoured the pictures which told a story. One of the most popular painters of the day was Millais, and a copy of his painting 'The Order of Release', was to be seen in many homes. He belonged to a group of artists, among them Burne-Jones and Holman Hunt, who called themselves 'Pre-Raphaelites', because they admired very much the work of the artists who had lived before the time of Raphael. They

Above: 'My First Sermon', by Millais.

Left: 'The Order of Release' by Millais, the Victorian painter.

146

'My Second Sermon'.
The novelty has now
worn off! Victorians liked
series of paintings which
told a story.

Right: 'King Cophetua and
the Beggar Maid' by Burne-
Jones. The painting is an
example of the Victorian
romantic love of the past.

took infinite pains over the detail of their pictures, went in for bright colours and showed great skill. They, like the architects, looked back to the Middle Ages for their inspiration. They saw it as a time when artists and craftsmen worked together to create things of beauty. They did not see anything exciting or inspiring in the nineteenth century of machines and machine-made goods. Because so many things made by machines were ugly, they thought that everything mechanical must be ugly. They did not realize the possibilities which lay in the machines. They never dreamed that beautiful designs could be carried out by such means, or that machines themselves could be beautiful.

Attempts were made to go back to hand weaving. Though working at a craft like this may give a great deal of pleasure to people who enjoy it, and may produce beautiful results, it was impossible to stop the growth of machinery and in spite of the efforts of some of the artists to halt its progress, more and more work was done by machinery rather than by hand.

Entertainments

For middle-class families there were fewer entertainments outside the home than there are now, and more inside the home. People made their own amusements in the evenings. There would be games of all kinds, perhaps reading aloud, or music. All girls who had any musical ability (and some who had not) learned to play the piano. The Dickens

A middle-class family entertain themselves at home.

children (there were nine of them), used to get up charades and have impromptu dances when their friends came in. It was an age of large families and there was generally one member at least who could entertain the others with a song.

Lucky children might be taken to the pantomime at Christmas; otherwise to go to the theatre was a rare pleasure. At Christmas there were always parties for the children and dances for the young people.

There was more leisure when so much of the burden of housekeeping was left to servants. The publishers provided reading material in the shape of weekly and monthly magazines for old and young, for boys and girls. In 1855 the stamp duty was taken off periodicals and this together with improved printing made the magazines cheaper.

They provided stories, accounts of foreign places, descriptions of new inventions and news from all parts of the world. In one very popular journal, *The Englishwoman's Domestic Magazine*, there were also recipes for the cook, news of the latest fashions from Paris, and advice given on all the problems which beset the lady in charge of the household. The children's magazines told their young readers how to look after their pets, how to make toys, and there were plenty of hair-raising stories long before the Westerns came in. In fact they were very much like the magazines of today except that the illustrations were not photographs, but steel engravings, and perhaps we might find the language a little stilted.

Fashions 1860. A plate from the *Englishwoman's Domestic Magazine*.

Church on Sunday.

Most of the novelists of that day published their books as serials in some journal. That is perhaps not the best way of writing a novel. For the editor of the magazines it had one great advantage. If he had managed to get hold of an author who could write a lively story, he knew the public would be eager to buy the next instalment, so he was sure of a steady sale. Dickens published in this way. He followed very carefully the public reaction to each chapter. If he found the interest was flagging a little, he would next week introduce a new character or else switch the story to something more exciting. When he found some of his readers were getting a bit bored with Martin Chuzzlewit, he sent him off to America. If you want to read a novel of Dickens now, you can take it off the shelf and read it from cover to cover. At the time when he was writing them you would have to wait a whole week before you found out what was happening to Little Nell or Oliver Twist.

When the novel was published in book form it was expensive. The cost of a good-sized novel was 30s., a great sum in those days. That was too much for most people, so we get the circulating libraries which supplied the novels to their subscribers. There were no public libraries as there are now.

On one day of the week there was no entertainment at all: that was Sunday. On that day everything except the churches and the chapels was closed. In strict families, and many of them were strict, all toys and books were put away and no games of any kind could be played.

A stroll in the park.

Foreigners reported with amazement on the empty streets and the general air of solemnity and dullness.

It was not so bad for those who could enjoy themselves for the other six days of the week, but for the working-class it meant that they never even had a chance to see a museum or a picture gallery. Finally, after a number of petitions had been sent to the Home Secretary, bands were allowed to play in the parks on Sundays. This move was vigorously opposed by Lord Shaftesbury, who, though he had fought hard for shorter hours of work in the factories and for early closing on Saturday, could not reconcile himself to allowing any ordinary pleasure on Sunday. Towards the end of the century conditions were much less strict.

There was more interest, too, in outdoor sport. The gentle game of croquet gave way to the more strenuous game of tennis. This had one great advantage in that in time it freed women from wearing long heavy skirts, though if you look at a photograph of early tennis players you will think they look pretty uncomfortable. Cycling became popular and was an even greater influence for female independence and lighter clothing, and before the roads were jammed with motor-cars it was a delightful way of exploring the countryside.

Two great outdoor sports became an established feature of our national life during the later part of the nineteenth century – football and cricket. It is now very nearly one hundred years since the first 'Cup Final'. Originally only fifteen teams competed, all from the south

Women playing tennis in 1882.

of England; but northern teams then proceeded to win the cup for nearly twenty years, until in 1901 the 'Spurs' brought the cup south again. The English Rugby Union was also founded nearly one hundred years ago, and before the end of the century not only had the game become thoroughly established in Wales, Scotland and Ireland, but also English teams were already visiting Australia and New Zealand.

It was only at the very end of our period that large numbers of people started to watch football matches. But cricket had already become popular, and the attendance at the very first 'Test Match' between **England and Australia in 1877** (which was played in Melbourne) was high even by the standards of today. Originally football was entirely an amateur game, and the professional footballer, playing the game for money, was unheard of until the 1880s, but county cricket clubs already included a large number of professionals. Indeed, there was once a 'strike' just before a Test Match against Australia, when five leading cricketers demanded £20 if they were to play, instead of the £10 which they had been offered.

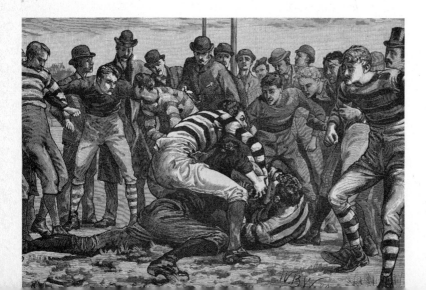

Rugby football in 1882

More freedom for girls

Children in middle-class families were strictly controlled by their parents, more particularly by fathers because they held the purse strings. The daughters had less freedom than their brothers. When the sons left school they went out into the world to earn their living and become independent. The daughters stayed at home to help their mothers entertain and to wait there until they married. This does not mean that the girls were all unhappy. Often they had a jolly, lively home and did not want to leave it. However, they did not all get married, and many of them longed to get out into the world and do something interesting and useful.

Florence Nightingale had to struggle hard before she was able to learn nursing. There were two difficulties young women had to face if they carried their point and tried to enter a profession. Their fathers thought it was undignified if the daughters worked. Only poor girls worked. A father would say proudly 'I can support my daughters, they have no need to work;' though illogically he might groan when the dressmaker's bills came in. The second difficulty was the current idea that it was 'unwomanly' for a woman to want to push her way in the world. Tennyson wrote *The Princess*, and said: 'He for the sword, for the needle she.' It is hard to argue against a prejudice like this. Fortunately some men and women thought it was important that girls should be educated just as boys were. A group of women went to see the examiners at Cambridge to ask if girls could be entered for the local examinations (something like our G.C.E.). Miss Emily Davies, who was the spokesman, was so nervous lest she did not put the case properly that she could not keep back a tear. The examiners gave their consent and one of them said afterwards that he had agreed because when he saw tears in Miss Davies's eyes, he knew she must be a 'truly womanly woman'.

The next hurdle to cross was the entrance to the universities, and after some years women gained the right of studying for degrees.

The hardest fight was over the career of medicine. That, everyone thought, was going a little too far. Nursing, after all, was womanly, and if girls really wanted to study, it might be allowed, but to study medicine was indecent, and the colleges which granted the medical degrees refused to permit women to enter for their examinations. Some few bold women persisted. A friendly professor in Edinburgh, Professor Simpson, agreed that women could come to his lectures. Led by Sophia Jex-Blake, a hardy little band went to Edinburgh and presented themselves at the first lecture. The men students brought in a sheep which they pushed to the front of the class. When the Professor asked them why they had brought it, they replied: 'We understand the lower animals can now study medicine.' 'The animal has more sense than those who brought it in,' the Professor replied, coldly. On the way home from the lectures the women were pelted with eggs and stones by the men students. Finally the London School of Medicine was founded in

London for women medical students. These pioneers had a tough fight. Often their families disapproved of them. They had to put up with many slights and sneers.

By the end of the nineteenth century women had won their right of entry to all courses in the universities.

The campaign they had fought led to another one. Why, some of the women asked, were they not allowed to vote? The story of how they struggled for that will be told in the next volume.

Village life

If a man, born in 1800 in London or any provincial town, had gone back after long absence to the place of his birth, he would probably not have been able to recognize it and would have lost himself in a labyrinth of streets unknown to him. If he had been born in a village, he might have found on his return that it had changed comparatively little. There might still be the picturesque thatched cottages, the old church, the elm trees in the churchyard, and few new buildings. While new industries sprang up in the towns in the nineteenth century, in the village the only occupation remained farming.

Though the villages might look romantic and innocent, life for the farm-worker was hard and unrewarding. The older men remembered the better days before the Napoleonic wars.

An Essex village in about 1836.

154

Come all ye bold Britons where'er you may be,
I pray give attention and listen to me.
There once was good times but they've gone now complete,
For a poor man now lives on eight shillings a week.

In the reign of old George as you all understand,
There then was contentment throughout the whole land.
Each poor man could live and get plenty to eat,
And now he must pine on eight shillings a week.

Our venerable fathers remember the year
When a man earned three shillings a day and his beer.
He then could live well, keep his family neat.
Now he must live on eight shillings a week.

There was violence sometimes in these villages. After the introduction of the mechanical threshing machine, which took away from the labourer the chance to earn extra money by threshing, there were riots in the southern counties. They were put down with severity by the Whig government.

The poachers

There was one source of food which was jealously guarded by the land-owner – that was game – hares, pheasants, partridges and the humble

A mechanical threshing machine.

rabbit. No one but the lord of the manor had the right to kill them. Gamekeepers went armed and spring-guns were put in the woods to trap the unwary. When a man had a hungry family to feed, the temptation to snare a rabbit and beat up the gamekeeper was great. Men went out at night with snares, and there were fights between the poachers and the gamekeepers. The poacher had a good chance of getting off and escaping capture, or there might be a lenient magistrate. A warning verse said:

> Come all you gallant poachers that ramble free from care,
> That walk out on moonlight nights with dog and gun and snare,
> The jolly hares and pheasants you have at your command,
> Not thinking that your last career is in Van Diemen's Land.

If you have read *Vanity Fair* you may remember how Sir Pitt Crawley learned that his second gamekeeper had been 'whipped nigh to death' because he had been caught on someone else's ground.

Conditions improve

By the middle of the century wages had risen, and life was more comfortable for the farm-worker, especially in the north where there was always the possibility of working in a factory, and the farmers therefore had to pay higher wages. Women and children worked too; after the harvest they gleaned and often got enough corn to supply the family with bread for a few months. Children helped in potato-digging. To the

Gamekeepers *(far left)* and gleaners.

156

'Harvest Home'.

townsman the life of the country worker seemed dull and monotonous. W. H. Hudson talked to an old shepherd who told him about his life. 'Fifty years,' he said,

I've been on the downs and fields, day and night, seven days a week, and I've been told it's a poor way to spend a life, working seven days for ten or twelve or at most thirteen shillings a week. But I've never seen it like that; I like it and I always did my best. You see, Sir, I always took a pride in it. I never left a place but I was asked to stay. When I left it was because of something I didn't like. I couldn't never abide cruelty to dog or beast. And I couldn't abide bad language. If my master swore at the sheep or dog I wouldn't bide with he, no not for a pound a week. I liked my work and I liked knowing about sheep. Not things in books, for I never had no books, but what I found out with my own sense if you understand me.

There may have been many who felt like that.

Village crafts

At one time there had been many crafts practised in the country. People made their own furniture; there was spinning and weaving and clock-making. With the coming of machinery this sort of work died out. But many traditions lingered on. May Day was kept, though it was only a shadow of the festival it had been. To the end of the century the mummers went round on Christmas Eve to act the play of St George and the Dragon. The end of the harvest meant 'Harvest Home'; a good meal was provided by the farmer with plenty to eat and drink. Country dancing was forgotten and the church choirs gave up having local musicians with violins. Smocks were worn by the men on Sunday, and the beautiful work which went into their making was one of the last traditional crafts to survive. England in the nineteenth century became a country of town-dwellers, with a few areas where the old customs and dialects lingered.

The greatness of the Victorians

The Victorians are sometimes despised as being dull and stuffy, but we can see from this chapter that they were energetic people who began the struggle for many advantages which have since been won and which we now take for granted. They passed the first laws to make town life healthy, and it was Victorian women who founded the nursing profession and won the right for women to go to universities. We shall see in the next volume how in the twentieth century other people built upon the foundations they had laid.

Dates to remember

1835   Municipal Corporations Act
1848   Public Health Act
1875   Artisans' Dwellings Act

Things to do

For this chapter go to your local library and get as much information as you can about your town.
1   Find out about when public services were introduced: water, sewage, gas and electricity.
2   How much are your local rates and on what are they spent?
3   Look round your streets and notice what houses were built in the Victorian Gothic style. Often the name of the street gives a clue to when it was built.

Things to discuss

Have we lost more than we have gained by becoming town-dwellers?

Books to read

J. Kamm, *How Different from us,* Bodley Head
M. R. Mitford, *Our Village,* Dent
Peter Moss, *Sports and Pastimes through the Ages,* Harrap
M. and A. Potter, *Houses,* Murray
F. Gordon Roe, *The Victorian Child,* Phoenix House
F. Thompson, *Lark Rise to Candleford,* Oxford University Press
R. J. Unstead, *A History of Houses,* Black

Come all ye bold Bri-tons where 'er you may be, I
pray give at- ten-tion and lis-ten to me, There
once was good times but they've gone now com- plete, For a
poor man now lives on eight shil-lings a week.

Come, all you gal-lant poach-ers, that ram-ble free from
care, That walk out on moon-light nights with
dog, and gun, and snare; The jolly hares and phea-sants you
have at your com- mand, Not think-ing that your
last ca-reer is in Van Die-men's Land.

Chapter 10
Science, inventions and education

Darwin

Exciting discoveries were made in the nineteenth century. Historians and archaeologists dug up the remains of ancient cities and tried to find the secrets of age-old forgotten civilizations. Geologists studied the earth itself and found much to puzzle them in the formation of coral islands, volcanoes, and the curious formation of the rocks in which they found fossilized animals embedded. It had always been accepted that the world as we know it was 6,000 years old; this was by the Bible reckoning. But in Victorian times the geologists found evidence that there had been an ice age and that once the northern hemisphere had been covered with ice. All this pointed to the theory that the earth was millions of years old, and that it had taken countless ages for the rocks and mountains to achieve their present form.

There was interest, too, in the plants and animals which abounded in the world. Expeditions were sent out to report on discoveries in Australia and South America. One of the most famous of these expeditions is the voyage of the *Beagle*, a sailing ship which was sent out in 1831 to explore the coast of South America and to bring back an account of the plants and animals of that country.

The man who made this voyage so famous was Charles Darwin. He was the son of a doctor in Shrewsbury and as a boy had been looked on by his family as unlikely to turn out a success in anything. His hobbies seemed to his relations to be rather curious. At one time he had a passion for collecting all the beetles he could find. One day when he was in the woods, with a different beetle in each hand, he found a third kind. Not wanting to miss this and not having a hand free, he popped one beetle into his mouth. Certainly a boy who behaved like this was an oddity. He studied medicine in Edinburgh for a short time, then went to Cambridge where he continued to follow up his interest in natural history. When the *Beagle* was fitted out and a naturalist was wanted, someone suggested the young Charles Darwin, because fortunately his teachers had a higher opinion of him than his family had. His father's consent was given rather grudgingly, and on 27 December 1831 he sailed with the *Beagle* from Plymouth on a voyage which was to last five years.

Darwin soon forgot his seasickness in the excitement of his discoveries. He had every quality which a collector needs. He was thorough, exact and painstaking. He sent back his notes and specimens to his colleagues in England and was surprised when, at the end of the voyage, he found he had made a tremendous reputation for himself. Naturalists in the past had also made careful studies of animals, but

Charles Darwin.

160

The *Beagle*, with Darwin on board, on its voyage to South America and Australia, 1831–6.

they had thought that the species had never varied, that the animals they found had existed in that same form since the beginning of time. Darwin began to question this. He noticed a large number of animals which were nearly, but not quite, alike. On one island there might be an animal with certain features and on another island fifty miles away, there was the same animal but with a certain feature slightly modified. Could it be that these animals had all descended from one common ancestor and over the years had grown slightly different? And if so why had these differences appeared? Darwin had a book to read while on the voyage, a book on geology by Lyell, one of the first men to write about the probable age of the earth. If, thought Darwin, it had taken millions of years to form the rocks, had it perhaps also taken millions of years for animals to evolve into their present form?

The idea of evolution (which is gradual change) was not a new one. The Greeks had thought of it, so had Erasmus Darwin, the grandfather of Charles, and also the Frenchman, Lamarck. It is one thing to have an idea; we can all of us guess and sometimes make a lucky guess. It is quite another thing to produce a proof of the correctness of that idea. Darwin thought he had that proof in his notebooks. He saw that all animals had a struggle to survive. Those which were best at surviving their environment passed on the good qualities which had helped them to their descendants. This was called 'the survival of the fittest'. For example, in a cold climate, those who have the warmest fur will

Darwin noticed these finches on the Galápagos islands, off the South American coast. Some were nearly, but not quite, alike. Their beaks were different: one *(far left)* was adapted to seed-eating; another *(far right)* to insect-eating.

live. Darwin believed that this necessity for an animal to deal with its environment explained the immense variety of creatures.

Darwin was lucky in one way. He did not need to earn his living and so could retire quietly to a little village in Kent and study all the observations he had made at leisure, and publish a book when he had completed his work. He discussed his theories with other scientists, but did not bring out his famous book *The Origin of Species* until 1859. It hit the public like a bombshell. They might be prepared to accept the idea that animals had evolved, but Darwin placed man among the animals, and said that man developed from some ape-like ancestor. The debates were fast and furious. Man in his evolution had grown a brain which could not only think, but knew how to pass on knowledge. This, people said, placed man in a special class. It was a long time before the idea was accepted that man, as well as animals, was part of a slow evolutionary process. Perhaps it was humiliating for men to think they were related – even distantly – to apes. There was another side to this suggestion. If man had evolved to such a clever creature, to what heights could he not reach in the next million years? It was unlikely that evolution had stopped abruptly in the middle of the nineteenth century. So if Darwin brought man off his pedestal, he also held out a dazzling prospect for the future.

Of course, some of what Darwin wrote has been modified as new knowledge came to light. That does not diminish the importance of his work. His main idea, that man evolved from lower kinds of life, is still accepted.

A *Punch* cartoon ridicules the idea of man being related to apes. Alarmed flunkey: 'Mr G–G–G–O–O–ORILLA!'

Inventions

Have you ever been told how lucky you are to be young now, and what a lot of things you have which your elders did not have? The answer may be that what people do not know about, they never miss. If they were brought up with oil lamps they would not pine for the electric light they never knew. That is, of course, true, but nevertheless men from the beginning have tried to improve things, to invent new and better and more convenient ways of working.

What makes men want to invent? Sometimes it is sheer necessity. When timber for firewood became scarce, coal had to be mined, and methods of deep mining were developed. Wars and scarcity have often goaded men into finding some substitute for a commodity they could no longer obtain.

Some inventors have been lucky; they have hit on something which the world immediately wanted and have made fortunes for themselves. Others have worked all their lives, slaved away with determination, losing all their money in an effort to solve some puzzle connected with their work, and perhaps died in poverty (and been famous after their death) or been cheated out of their reward.

During all the centuries since the Romans left Britain in AD 410, very little technical progress was made until the eighteenth century. One invention depends on another. James Watt could not make his steam engine until the craft of rivet- and boiler-making had advanced. Pasteur could not have made his discoveries until the art of grinding lenses had been perfected. In the nineteenth century one invention

Bessemer steel plant about 1860. This invention by Bessemer for smelting steel helped to expand the industrial revolution.

Above left: A sailing ship. One of the clippers used on the China run.

Below left: A sailing ship with auxiliary steam engine, voyaging from London to New York.

followed rapidly after another. This was because new sources of power had been found. Until the eighteenth century power meant either man-power, horse-power, or wind or water. Once steam had been discovered, then the possibilities before people seemed limitless.

Transport

If we compare life in 1800 with life in 1900 perhaps the change which is most striking is the difference in the speed of communications. Schemes which helped industry were eagerly taken up by the manu-facturers, and at the same time they were of great importance in every-day life. Roads were first improved for the benefit of carrying goods, and the same is true of railways. Apart from their usefulness to industry, they made it easier for people to travel. When steam replaced sail on the high seas the same thing happened. When a mother said good-bye to her son in 1800 before he went to India she might have to wait for a year before she heard of his safe arrival. After the introduction of steam-ships and after the cutting of the Suez Canal (in 1869), the voyage to India lasted six weeks. The journey across the Atlantic was reduced from ten weeks to a fortnight. It no longer seemed a tremendous and rather terrifying adventure if a member of the family went east or west in search of work.

Telegraph

Messages used to be sent by lighting fires on the tops of high hills. These were used in times of war. When there was a fear of the invasion of England by Napoleon these beacons were kept in readiness to inform the country that the enemy had landed. It was reckoned that the whole country would get the message within twenty-four hours. But the only information which could be passed in this way was of a warning of danger. Napoleon used what was called a Chappe telegraph system; between Strasburg and Paris high posts were erected at intervals of six miles. On the tops of these posts were lamps which were turned according to a complicated system of signals and long messages were sent in this way. It was a most expensive method; besides the building of the posts, men had to be kept at each one, and to have covered the country with this apparatus would have been too costly to be practical. A German scientist first thought of using electric wires to pass mes-sages. When a scientifically-minded Russian showed it to the Tsar Alexander I, the latter forbade him even to write about it, because such speedy communication might weaken his authority in his empire. However, an Englishman visiting Germany heard about it and was much impressed and developed the electric telegraph system. In 1844 the first line from Slough to Paddington was opened and people were invited to come and inspect the 'wonder of the ages'. Its usefulness was demonstrated on 1 January 1845 when the operator at Paddington received this telegram:

Chappe telegraph post.

165

Early morse machine.

a murder has just been committed at salthill and the suspected murderer was seen to take a first class ticket to london by the train which left slough at 742 am he is in the garb of a kwaker with a brown greatcoat which reaches nearly down to his feet he is in the last compartment of the second first class carriage

The puzzled operator telegraphed back to know the meaning of 'kwaker' and was told that there was no sign on the telegraph panel for the letter which was between p and r. The man at Paddington walked round to the police station and two plain-clothes men saw the suspect get off the train. They followed him by horse-bus and arrested him. His name was John Tawell and when he was convicted and executed, the Londoners said: 'Them cords (the telegraph wires) have hung John Tawell.' An American called Morse invented the code which is called after him. It was a tremendous improvement on the first rather complicated system of signalling; this dot and dash method conquered the world.

The Tsar was not the only one who was afraid of the telegraph. Old people thought that it took all the goodness out of the air. They suspected it had connexions with the Evil One. In America, the enraged farmers of Kentucky tore down all the posts because they said: 'There ain't been a good crop since them wires was set up.'

In 1851 the cable was laid under the English Channel. In 1858 the first cable was laid under the Atlantic, but it broke down, and it was not until 1866 that there was a dependable connexion between America and Europe. The telegraph boy in blue uniform, carrying buff-coloured envelopes, became a common sight. Now good news, the birth of a baby, or bad news, the illness of a friend, could be learned in a few hours or less.

Telephone

A later wonder was the telephone. A German schoolmaster called Reis

166

Bell's telephone in operation.

London Central Telephone Office in 1883. The exchanges were operated chiefly by women.

first tried experiments in this line. He had a little workshop in the school yard where he tinkered with his models and showed them to the boys. No one took much notice of his invention even though he demonstrated it before a meeting of scientists. Later a Scottish-born American, Alexander Graham Bell, took up the idea and after years of experimenting produced an instrument which could pass on the human voice. This was in 1875. The following year he visited England and showed his apparatus to Queen Victoria, who took an immediate fancy to it and had a telephone installed between Osborne (her home in the Isle of Wight) and London. Soon exchanges were set up in all the principal cities of Great Britain. You could now actually hear the voice of your friend. If you wanted to fetch the doctor at night, you no longer had to throw gravel at his window to make him hear; you simply had to lift a telephone receiver.

Lighting

Not only could people communicate with each other more quickly; they could now, thanks to electricity, see more clearly. In 1800 rich people had used candles made of wax, and oil lamps. These were too expensive for the poor. They used a cheap kind of candle made from tallow. If you went out into the street at night you carried a lantern with you.

A Scotsman called Murdock, who was working in Cornwall, noticed that if coal were heated in a cauldron it gave out a bright flame. He built a large cauldron in his garden and cleverly piped the gas from this into his house for lighting. Every evening the citizens of Redruth came to gaze at the wonderful sight; the whole house was flooded with this bright light, so much brighter than the mellow beam of an oil lamp. Manufacturers soon saw the advantage of this. Men who worked the machinery needed lighting, and by using gas they were able to work through the night, and at a time when the demand for goods was high, it gave additional profit to have a night shift as well as a day shift. Gas lighting was introduced into London in 1809, and for the first time Londoners could go out into the streets and see their town bathed in light. This did not please everyone. One complaint in a newspaper said that it 'intervened in the Divine order of things which had made the night a darkness only to be relieved by the moon.' There were always some people who found extraordinary objections to anything new. It was

Gas lighting in Pall Mall in 1809 attracts a crowd of spectators.

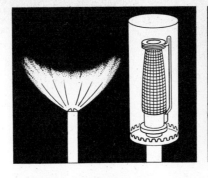

Four types of lighting.
From left to right: gas burners –
fishtail and Welsbach mantle;
electric light bulbs –
Edison 1879, and gas-filled
lamp.

some time before gas was brought into the houses. The first burners were called 'fishtail', because they spread out in that shape. Housewives complained that the gas was dirty and ruined the ceilings, but by the use of gas they were freed from the trouble of cleaning lamps.

At the end of the nineteenth century Edison, the American, found a method of making electric light bulbs. These were both cleaner and brighter than gas, and they needed no matches.

One great advantage of having the streets lit was that they became safer to walk in at night. Pickpockets and cut-throats could not so easily hide away. It is difficult to imagine what it must have been like to have to stumble around at night in dark unlit streets, and in moving about the house at night, always to have to carry a candle.

Electric street lighting in
London, 1881.

A daguerreotype family group in about 1857. People complained of the lack of colour, so some photographs were tinted by hand.

Photography

An invention which brought a great deal of pleasure and interest was that of the camera. At the end of the eighteenth century a daughter of the Duke of Hamilton decided to clean the old family portraits. When she removed the pictures from their frames, she found they were impressed on the paper, which was used for backing, quite accurately, and in two colours, purple and blue. The paper contained silver nitrate. She showed these papers to the Royal Society. They aroused some interest. In the meantime, a Frenchman called Daguerre was working out a plan by which he could get a picture printed on a piece of metal; these pictures were called after him 'daguerreotypes'. But only one could be made; it was not possible to make copies of them, and the sitter had to wait for thirty minutes in strong sunlight before plates were finished. He used a substance called silver iodide. The same year, 1839, that he brought out this new machine, a young Englishman, Fox-Talbot, was holidaying in Italy by Lake Como. He thought how wonderful it would be if that glorious view could somehow be captured and put on paper. When he returned to England he worked at his home in Wiltshire and finally brought out the modern camera, which, unlike the daguerreotype, could turn out any number of copies from one plate.

The people who suffered from this invention were the portrait

Daguerreotype camera of about 1840.

170

A street photographer of the 1890s.

painters. In the past they had gone round the country and offered to paint the family portraits. In the *Vicar of Wakefield* we read how one of these artists came round and painted the family at 15s. a head, with as many sheep thrown in as there was room for. However, most of these artists bought cameras and became photographers. For the historian who was interested in the past it was wonderful to have an exact and accurate picture of both places and people. If the camera had existed in the sixteenth century Henry VIII would never have been deceived about the beauty of Anne of Cleves. Naturally, as time went on, cameras were produced more cheaply, until at the end of the century small box cameras could be bought for 5s. We have a rough idea of what Queen Elizabeth looked like from portraits and flattering descriptions, but we know exactly what Queen Victoria looked like. At first in some books the photographs were pasted in; then later in 1880 the photographs themselves were printed in the books. Before this, illustrations had been steel engravings. Copies of famous pictures were made in this way. The camera made a better copy and provided a clearer idea of what the picture really looked like. A new industry grew up – that of picture-postcard making. At the end of the century, every middle-class family had its photograph album. It was a source of pleasure to look at the snapshots of friends and to be reminded of happy holidays in the past.

.*Left:* A 'hobby horse'.

Below: A penny-farthing bicycle, so-called because of the sizes of its wheels.

Bicycles

Another invention which brought enjoyment to the multitude was that of the bicycle. At the beginning of the century rude little boys in Mannheim jeered at the comic figure of Baron von Sauerbronn, dressed in a long green coat and top-hat, as he propelled himself along on what he called a riding horse, a vehicle of two wheels on which he sat and pushed himself forward. The idea behind this was that a great deal of energy was used up when walking by throwing the weight of the body from one side to the other. The Baron wanted to invent a method of keeping the body still. This horse, afterwards called a 'hobby horse', became a popular sport in both England and France, although no one thought of it seriously as a means of transport. Then MacMillan, a blacksmith in Dunfermline, improved on it by fixing levers on to the back wheel; a German then put levers on the front wheel and finally a Frenchman arranged the pedals between the wheels. A Swiss thought of the chain. So we can call this a real international invention. In England they were quite correctly called 'boneshakers'; riding with hard wheels on cobblestones could hardly be comfortable. Finally, the modern type of bicycle was manufactured by an Englishman. It was called the 'safety bicycle'. The wheels were the same size and much smaller than those of the boneshaker, and the wheels had hard rubber tyres. These machines were a great success and bicycle races became all the rage. A little boy of twelve in Belfast, called John Dunlop, asked his father to help him win a race. His father cut two pieces of garden hose, joined them together and blew up the tube and put it round the wheel in place of solid rubber tyres. John Dunlop sped away and easily won. From this moment, with pneumatic tyres, bicycles were not only safe, but also comfortable. They were certainly the most

A cycling scene in the 1890s. The cycles are all 'safety bicycles'.

democratic means of transport, used by prince and pauper. They soon became cheap enough to be within the reach of almost everyone. They helped to free women from their restrictions. They were obliged to wear more comfortable and looser clothes if they were to ride a bicycle. People who at the beginning of the century would never have been able to afford to ride a horse, or even to travel far by coach, now could go out at weekends and explore the countryside.

Other inventions helped people indirectly by making goods cheaper. The Bessemer process of making steel (invented by a German settled in England) reduced the price of steel. New methods of dyeing invented by Perkin reduced the price of cloth. Sewing-machines came from America so now girls would no longer have to spend long hours hemming sheets and making underclothes. Steel pens replaced quill pens. The typewriter was another invention which came to us from America. We could make a long list of ingenious devices which saved people time and made goods cheaper. If we summed all this up, we could say that at the end of the century life went at a quicker pace, travel was much faster and cheaper, and also that life was more interesting and more varied. There were more careers open to boys and also to girls. Books and magazines were available in greater variety.

Who were the people who designed all these fascinating wonders? First of all there were the scientists who did the research in mathematics, chemistry and physics. They explained the theories on which all the new work was based. Then many clever mechanics applied these theories, and found by trial and error how to improve the machines. But to make use of them all a whole army of skilled workers was needed; it was necessary that the men who operated the complicated machinery should understand it.

Need for education

But in 1850 half the population of England could neither read nor write. Not only were they cut off from the pleasure of reading books and magazines, but they could never do anything but unskilled work. In the modern world the demand for skilled workers was growing. If we think of the railways we can see that it was necessary for the ticket collectors to be able to read; for the stationmasters who had to send in reports, some kind of education was necessary. The telegraph system had to be operated, and the telephone exchanges had to be manned, all by the people who were literate, that is, who knew how to read. With the growth of business came the growth of offices and shops. Imagine going into a shop and finding the assistant could not write down your order or read the label on a bottle. The same thing was true of work in a factory. If a new machine was introduced, the engineer in charge of it would have to read the instructions which came with it. We can think of a hundred jobs which would be impossible for an illiterate.

Schools and technical colleges

At the beginning of the nineteenth century, upper- and middle-class children were educated because their parents could pay for it. There was no education for children whose parents could not pay. This was not true of all other countries; some governments saw to it that there were primary schools everywhere. But in England money was made out of the work of children and also there was the idea that people should not be given anything they did not pay for. Many people, too, were afraid of the working-class learning too much. After the French wars, when there was great distress and the government was afraid of disturbances, they thought men would be easier to control if they were ignorant.

But such a state of affairs could not go on. The children in our towns were growing up like savages. On Sundays, when the factories were closed and the children let loose, neither people nor property were safe. What was to be done? A wonderful invention provided the answer.

Lancastrian schools

A man named Lancaster, who loved children and thought that they had a right to be educated, opened a school in his father's sieve-making factory in Southwark. Children came along in hundreds and begged to be taught. He could not bear to turn them away. But he had no money to pay teachers, so he got older children to teach the younger ones, and found that in this way he could manage to teach 500 boys and girls with only one teacher. The children who did the teaching were called monitors. Some of them were only eight years old. Each monitor had ten pupils.

You can see in this picture what these schools looked like. When you visited one you heard a deafening noise and saw a bewildering

A Lancastrian school.

amount of movement. But really it was all as orderly as a military parade. At a signal the monitors went up to the platform and a teacher taught them something such as 'CAT spells cat'. Then the monitors went back to their group and put up a signal when every member had learned it.

These schools were more kind and cheerful places than you might expect. Punishments were mild for those days; for instance anyone who came to school dirty might have his face washed in front of the whole school. The children were given prizes for good work. Much of what they learned must have been extremely dull, learning by heart answers to questions. Here is an example of a lesson for older children:

Monitor	What have you been reading about?
Boy	Ruminating animals.
Monitor	Another name for ruminating?
Boy	Cud chewing
Monitor	What is the root of the word?
Boy	'Rumen' the cud.
Monitor	What does the termination 'ate' mean?
Boy	To do or to act in some way.
Monitor	Ruminate is then –
Boy	To act on the cud.

What do you think of that sort of education?

Left: A one-room school. The tall girls standing up *(left)* are monitors.

State education

Parents paid only a few pennies a week if they sent a child to one of these schools. That may sound a small sum; but remember that the wages of most workers at this time were often not more than 18s. or £1 a week, and if a man had several children he would not be able to send them all to school. Perhaps these schools were important because they were so cheap that the government could afford to encourage education of this kind. You may remember that in Chapter 3 we noticed that the Whig government of 1832 was ready to consider new ideas. In 1833 Parliament voted £20,000 towards the cost of maintaining those schools. (That same year it spent £30,000 on rebuilding the stables of Buckingham Palace.) The sum it granted to the schools was not large but it was the thin end of a very big wedge. Every year the grant was given and was gradually increased. Finally in 1870 an act was passed which ordered the local councils to set up schools in places where there were not sufficient schools for the children. This does not mean that after 1870 every child went to school. In the first place the schools had to be built and then teachers had to be found. In 1891 all these schools were made free and attendance at them was compulsory. No longer would the government allow children to grow up completely ignorant.

Above right: Girls using bar bells in a gymnastics class at a Board school set up by the 1870 act.

Below right: Teaching staff of a school at the turn of the century.

Technical education

These two acts satisfied the most urgent need. More, however, was necessary. Men noticed with alarm that Germany was beginning to manufacture goods as well as, or better than we did, and also could sell them more cheaply. America, too, began to be a serious rival in trade. Why was this? We have noticed that this country had a tremendous advantage because it was the first to build steam engines and to manufacture goods with machinery. In that way we sold our goods everywhere and became 'the workshop of the world'. But this was also a disadvantage. The people who came after us had the benefit of our experience, and when the Germans made machines they were the latest models, an improvement on what we had done. An Englishman might find he was making quite a good profit from his old machinery and would hesitate before spending a lot of money on something newer and better. Or he might say, 'It will last my time.' Our coalmines were many of them nearly a hundred years old. Other countries were catching up and beginning to overtake us. One reason, as the businessmen of the Midlands and North realized, was that there was more money spent on technical education abroad. Germany and France had technical colleges where students were encouraged to study. Here in England we had left all that to chance. It was reported in 1870 that in Bradford, a town of half a million people, where prosperity depended on the development of the wool trade, there was only one class held on

A laboratory in Finsbury Technical College, 1884, which was one of the first technical schools.

technical subjects connected with the trade, and that was held once a week in a cellar. Although we had invented the process of aniline dyeing in England, it was developed in Germany. There were many other examples of German enterprise.

These facts led the businessmen to urge the setting up of technical colleges, and in the last twenty-five years of the century they were established in London and all the provincial towns. Later many of them became universities where all subjects were studied. People realized at last that if Britain were to hold her place, more people must be trained.

What an enormous change took place in a hundred years. When in 1805 a visitor asked Mr Wollaston, a scientist, if he might see his laboratory, Mr Wollaston rang the bell and asked the footman to bring it in on a tray. Compare that with the picture on the opposite page showing a laboratory in a technical college in 1884.

Dates to remember

1870   Education Act which said that there should be a school available for all children

1891   Primary education made free and compulsory

Things to do

1   Which of the inventions of the nineteenth century do you think have been most useful to the housewife?

2   Find out what is meant by patenting an invention.

3   Which is the oldest school in your neighbourhood? When was it built and by whom?

4   What subjects do you learn in school which you would not have learned a hundred years ago?

5   Find pictures of early railway engines and notice how the designs of engines improved in later years.

Most of the inventors led interesting lives. In Egon Larsen's *History of Invention*, published by Phoenix House, you can read about many of them.

Books to read

E. Larsen, *Men who shaped the Future*, Phoenix House

H. E. L. Mellersh, *Charles Darwin*, Barker

John Rowland, *Epics of Invention*, Werner Laurie

F. Sherwood Taylor, *A Century of Science*, Heinemann

F. Sherwood Taylor, *Illustrated History of Science*, Heinemann

H. Sootin, *Michael Faraday*, Blackie

Chapter 11
You and the doctor

What do we do if we feel ill or have a pain? We either visit the doctor or send for him. We expect him to know what is the matter with us. If he is not sure he may send us to the nearest hospital where we shall be examined by another doctor. If by any chance we have to have an operation, we need not be afraid of the pain involved, though we may dislike the idea of the discomfort. Nowadays we think it is the normal thing to be well and fit. If anything is wrong with us we are confident that it can be treated. It is a terrible shock to hear of the death of a baby or a small child. We do not expect young people to die.

At the beginning of the nineteenth century the prospect was different. We have no accurate information until 1837 when a register of births and deaths began to be kept, but some towns used to issue what were called 'Bills of Mortality'; these were lists of all the people who had died during the year, giving their ages and the cause of death, and from these we can make a rough estimate that at the turn of the nineteenth century two out of every five babies born alive died before they were five years old. In 1840 the average age of death is given as twenty-nine. That does not mean that most people died at that age; the average was so low because of the great number of very young children who died.

What were the diseases which carried them off? Again we cannot be accurate. Often the cause was put down simply as fever or swelling, without saying what particular fever. There were more killing diseases than we have now. Smallpox was one, typhoid, scarlet fever and diphtheria were others. There were outbreaks of cholera; 2,000 people died from this in one week in London. Tuberculosis was common, in those days called consumption. We notice there are many deathbed scenes in the novels of Dickens. We now think of his concentration on death as rather morbid, but then it was a reflection of what life was like. It often happened that a mother died in childbirth. A modern novelist would not now feel he was at liberty to kill off all his awkward characters as Dickens did. Think what a different outlook on life people must have had. There were more motherless children; the breadwinner of the family might die and leave his children destitute. A lot of ill health which might now be cured, was accepted then as inevitable.

The doctors

What about the doctors? There were then three kinds of doctors. There were the apothecaries, who prescribed drugs for their patients. They

An inmate of a lunatic asylum. In the early nineteenth century the mentally sick were chained up in cells and, since there was no idea of curing them, they received no medical treatment.

were not allowed to charge for giving advice, they could only charge for the medicines they sold, and this probably resulted in too many pills and draughts being ordered. They were ranked as much lower than the physicians. These latter, especially in London, were held in respect. There was always a physician attached to the court and in the eighteenth century many noblemen employed a private physician to be always in attendance. The surgeons were looked on as inferior to the physicians; this is probably because they worked with their hands (the word surgeon comes from the Greek words for hand and work), and also their work was rather like that of the butcher. We have the remains of the distinction to this day when we address a physician as Dr Smith and a surgeon as Mr Smith. In *Jane Eyre* we read of 'Mr Lloyd, an apothecary sometimes called in by Mrs Reed, if one of the servants were ailing; for herself and her children she employed a physician.' And in *Middlemarch,* a novel by George Eliot, Lady Chettam, talking of a new doctor who is said to belong to a good family: 'For my part I prefer a medical man to be more on a footing with the servants. He is often the cleverer.' A young man then who wanted to study medicine would be apprenticed to a doctor for five years and then attend lectures at a hospital. Of course, if he later had a country practice he would be expected to do everything, to be a bonesetter and to cure fevers.

How discoveries were made

Doctors are like other human beings. Some of them were good and conscientious, some were inclined to accept what they were taught without trying to find out anything more about their work. All of them were hampered by the fact that they did not know the cause of most diseases and if you do not know the cause it is not possible to treat an illness scientifically. Too often a traditional remedy was clung to, for example bleeding, and purging, which some doctors prescribed for almost every complaint. George Eliot describes two doctors in a town; one of them gives all his patients port wine to build them up, and the other resorts to bleeding to pull them down. Each doctor was sure his method was right. Some useful things were discovered by careful observation. For instance scurvy had been a disease which afflicted seamen who went on long voyages. It was found that when they were given fresh vegetables to eat they kept healthy. Captain Cook did not know why this happened but he knew it did, and at every port of call he took vegetables and fruit on board. After this was found out every ship of the Royal Navy had to have limejuice given out on board. Dr Jenner was an example of an observant doctor. He noticed that milkmaids never got smallpox. He asked himself the question: What is different about milkmaids? Why are they not like other people? He saw that they frequently had small spots on their hands; they contracted a disease called 'cow-pox' from milking the cows. This gave Jenner the idea that possibly one disease – and cow-pox was a very mild one – would prevent the other. He tried it out. He vaccinated people, which

meant that he injected a little of the cow-pox serum into a healthy person, and after that they were not in danger of catching smallpox. One mild disease prevented the worse one. When vaccination was accepted smallpox died out in England.

Another doctor who had this sort of inquiring mind was a certain Dr Snow. In a cholera outbreak he noticed that it was restricted to a very small neighbourhood of Tottenham Court Road. He visited all the houses where there were victims, inquired what they ate and what they drank. He found they all drew their water from the Broad Street pump. In the next street where they had a different source of water, no one had cholera. Then a case occurred in Highgate. Dr Snow went there. The woman concerned had had water brought her every day by carrier from the Broad Street pump, because she thought the water was so healthy. By this patient investigation Dr Snow found that cholera was carried by infected water. This was an important step towards getting rid of the disease.

When a doctor visits you now he pulls out a thermometer and stethoscope. The clinical thermometer was not invented until the middle of the nineteenth century, so a doctor had to measure the amount of fever by feeling the patient's forehead to determine whether the temperature was going up or down. A Frenchman, Laennec, invented the stethoscope in 1819. Laennec was a Breton of humble

A cartoon published by the Anti-Vaccine Society in 1802. It was thought that people who were vaccinated by being injected with cow-pox serum would develop cow-like characteristics.

182

Plague spot in South Lambeth.

parentage and extremely shy and retiring. One day he was called to attend a fashionable lady. It was the practice then for the doctor to press his ear to the chest of the patient to hear the heart beating. Laennec was embarrassed when he visited this lady who was not only aristocratic, but also extremely stout, and he hesitated before approaching this mountain of flesh. Then he remembered having seen two little boys in the country playing with a piece of wood which they had hollowed out. They were shouting through it. Laennec took some stiff cardboard, made a roll of it, applied one end to his patient's chest, and clearly heard through it the beating of the heart, because the sound was canalized. From this he developed the stethoscope.

Of course, observant doctors would notice that in crowded districts there were more epidemics than in the more airy neighbourhoods, but the connection between dirt and disease was not properly understood. The general idea was that there was some peculiar substance in the air they called 'miasma'; they associated this with the unpleasant smell which pervaded areas where there was a lot of sickness. For instance, they noticed that in marshy areas a complaint called ague was frequent. They attributed this to the bad, marshy air, *mal aria*, and called it malarial fever, from which we got the word malaria. As long as the cause of an illness was not known, treatment was often to be a hit or miss affair.

183

Hospitals

If you visit a friend in hospital now you find a clean, pleasant ward, warm and well ventilated. Your friend is being nursed by competent young women who are being taught how to nurse.

In 1800 there were two kinds of hospitals. There were the workhouses where the sick paupers had to go, and about them we have little real information. We can guess they were very bad because those who were ill were looked after by any paupers who were able to walk about, and many of these must have been old and infirm. As we saw in Chapter 3 there was a great anxiety to keep down the rates and not to spend money unnecessarily on paupers who were regarded as useless members of society. It was not until the second half of the century that reforms were made here, and proper nurses were appointed to what were called the Workhouse Infirmaries. The other kind of hospitals were the voluntary ones. These had been founded by charitable persons, sometimes as long ago as the sixteenth century and were meant for the sick poor. We have records of these which give us some idea of how they were organized.

If you went into a hospital ward at the beginning of the nineteenth century probably the first thing you would notice would be the famous 'hospital smell'. This was found in all hospitals at that time, not only in England. The sick often slept two in a bed, the sheets were not often washed – nor were the patients – and the windows were kept shut. Sometimes in the winter they would be boarded up. If you add to this that the

A ward in one of the better hospitals, Middlesex Hospital, 1808. There are open windows and a fire to heat the room.

ward was crowded, you can imagine that the smell would be unpleasant. The nurses were generally of a rather poor type, ignorant and dirty themselves. Dickens has left us a description of early Victorian nurses in his picture of Sairey Gamp and Betsey Prig. Nurses were supposed to attend to the patients, bring them food and wash the clothes. They did not do any dressings; this was done by the surgeons themselves or their 'dressers' who went round with them. The nurses were badly paid and there was little incentive to become a hospital nurse. They slept in the wards with the patients and cooked their own food. The general impression amongst the public was that nurses were rather a degraded sort of people. At night 'watchers' were employed to look after the patients. These were even more disreputable than the nurses; often they would come in to sleep off their drunkenness. On one occasion a doctor, seeing one of the watchers come in and prepare to lie down on a bed in the ward, thinking to shame her asked 'Are you not disturbed at the thought of all the patients you have to look after?' The woman thought he was kindly inquiring about the soundness of her sleep and answered cheerfully 'Oh, they don't disturb me.' Middle-class people never went into these hospitals, nor did the poor unless they had no relative to look after them. In one hospital no patient was admitted unless he brought with him the price of his burial. In conditions like this recovery was not very easy and one doctor said 'A soldier had more chance of survival on the field of Waterloo than a man who goes into hospital.'

We must beware of exaggeration. These were the worst conditions

Sairey Gamp and Betsey Prig in *Martin Chuzzlewit*, more occupied with drink than duty.

and some hospitals were better. When people want to reform an institution they paint its evils in dark colours. It is undeniable that nurses did drink a great deal, but so did most people at that time. The patients had two or three pints of beer a day. Then doubtless amongst the nurses there would be some who attended to their duties properly. Florence Nightingale said the best nurse she had was a Mrs Roberts from St Thomas's, who could neither read nor write. We may smile when we read that a matron was appointed because she was a widow in poor circumstances (no other recommendation seemed necessary), but she might turn out to be an excellent matron with a natural gift for nursing. The doctors, too, tried to get reliable women into the hospitals and tried to train them to carry out instructions. But even the best of hospitals must have been grim places.

An interest in nursing began to be aroused amongst middle-class women who had leisure and not sufficient occupation. The middle-classes were growing rich and their daughters were no longer completely occupied in household tasks as their grandmothers had been. Many wanted to do something useful and Florence Nightingale, whom you remember reading about in Chapter 5, made nursing a respectable and skilled profession for women.

But what if you had to have an operation in those days? There was no merciful anaesthetic to send you into a deep sleep. Surgeons then had to operate on their patients without anything to deaden the pain. Many

Nurses at St Thomas's Hospital, 1881. They are in uniform and give an impression of respectability and devotion to duty.

things had been tried, such as freezing the part which had to be cut or constricting it. Generally the patient was given plenty of brandy. No surgeon, unless he was an insensitive brute, could feel anything but horror at having to inflict the sort of pain caused by an operation. Some men were prevented from becoming doctors because of this. Young Charles Darwin, who was a medical student in Edinburgh, wrote:

I attended on two occasions the operating theatre and saw two very bad operations, one on a child, but I rushed out before they were completed. Nor did I ever attend again, for hardly any inducement could have been strong enough to make me do so. The two cases fairly haunted me for many a long year.

The restored operating theatre of old St Thomas's Hospital. Notice the box of sand underneath the table.

An operation then was only resorted to if the alternative was death or lifelong suffering. Most of them were amputation of limbs or cutting of growths. Not only was the surgeon feared almost as much as the hangman, but an operation was often followed by death from blood-poisoning a few days later. In some way not then understood a wound became septic and the patient would die.

It is understandable that when so much pain was involved a surgeon would aim to be as quick as possible. Some of them were marvellously skilful. Professor Syme of Edinburgh used to practise by sharpening pencils and shaving with the left hand in order to be able to use the maximum speed when he operated. A French surgeon used to walk from his home to the hospital carrying a lithotome (an instrument for removing stone from the bladder) in his left hand and picked out nuts with it from his coat pocket, to keep his fingers in practice. The passers-by just thought he was a harmless eccentric. This speed had a disadvantage, because not so much care could be taken.

The properties of laughing gas (nitrous oxide) had been discovered in the eighteenth century by Priestley, but the doctors had not thought of the idea of using it for their work. Faraday discovered that ether would put people to sleep, but again he did not see the importance of this. Another doctor did: Dr Hickman in Shropshire operated on animals after using ether. Unfortunately he died at the age of twenty-nine before he could arouse interest in this experiment. Finally, deliverance from pain came from America, where a dentist experimented with gas for extracting teeth. He then suggested using ether and it was first used in a hospital in Boston. The American, Dr Oliver Wendell Holmes, christened this form of insensibility 'anaesthesia'.

Ether had an unpleasant smell and was also an irritant. Simpson, the Professor of Midwifery in Edinburgh, tried chloroform, which he thought would be better than ether. He first tried it on animals and then had to experiment to find the amount which would be needed for human beings. One night he brought home two of his assistants to dinner, and told his wife she must leave them undisturbed after dinner for exactly two hours. What was her horror when she went into the dining-room two hours later and found all three men snoring heavily, leaning over the table, a small saucer in front of each of them. However, they

Simpson and his friends test chloroform.

recovered consciousness with no ill effects. Simpson began to use chloroform for women in labour, and by doing this he caused a great outcry, especially from the clergy. Did it not say in the Bible 'in sorrow shall she bring forth'? Simpson had a ready answer – he explained that the correct translation of the word was labour, not sorrow. One doctor told him it was interfering with a natural process and might cause death. 'My dear Doctor,' replied Simpson, 'why do you ride in a carriage and interfere with the natural process of walking? There are often accidents to carriages.' At last, when Queen Victoria was given chloroform for the birth of Prince Leopold, the practice was accepted. It is interesting to think that Simpson nearly gave up medicine, because like young Darwin, he could not bear to witness the pain involved in operations. He came from a poor family and when he remembered what sacrifices had been made for him, he decided it was his duty to carry on with his studies.

This great discovery meant that no longer would people have to endure agonizing pain. It also meant that surgeons would not need to work with such speed. Also many more operations could be attempted which could never have been done before. Anaesthesia was hailed as the greatest advance in surgery.

But alas for all the high hopes. The pain, it is true, was gone but the post-operation deaths were still there; in fact there were more deaths because there were more operations. Simpson realized that a mother who had her baby at home, even if that home was only one room, had more chance of surviving than if she went into hospital. Sir Frederick Treves, in his memoirs, remembered how when he explained to a woman how necessary it was to operate on her daughter, she replied 'I know it is necessary, but I don't know how we shall afford the funeral.' Surgeons then wore black gowns when they operated; these were not washed; and the surgeon would wipe his knife

Below: Snow's chloroform inhaler.

on his gown, and in going through the wards would examine one patient after another, carrying infection.

This problem of post-operation death exercised the mind of a young surgeon called Lister, who first worked under Syme in Edinburgh. He fought hard for cleanliness, and insisted that his dressers should wash their hands before they touched a patient, also that the bandages should be clean. Even then the results were discouraging. About 50 per cent of his cases died. The wound would appear to be healing, then on the fourth day fever would set in. The wound would putrefy and the patient died. One night he was walking with a friend at whose house he was going to dine; the friend remarked that he had read a paper in a French journal which might interest him, it was on the causes of putrefaction. When they arrived at the house Lister asked for the journal. 'Can't you wait until we have dined?' said the friend. 'I can,' answered Lister, 'but it will be very difficult.' The paper had been written by a Frenchman called Pasteur. He was a chemist, not a doctor. He had seen

One of the first operations performed under an anaesthetic in 1847. The surgeons are in their normal black suits and no masks are worn.

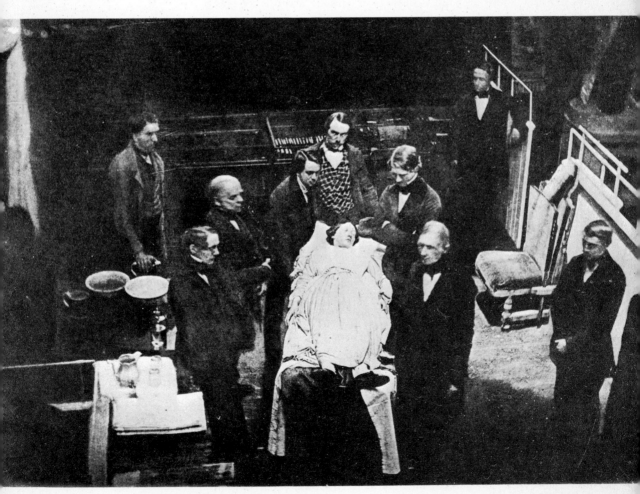

through his microscope small creatures he called germs, which were present everywhere and some of which were harmful. Lister read this with breathless excitement. If this were true, then it might explain the mystery why some of his patients died and others lived. Harmful germs might have entered the wound and caused the blood-poisoning. In that case something must be found which would kill the germs. He remembered that in the town of Carlisle they put carbolic on the refuse to prevent the smell. He went there to examine it. He first tried a new method on a man who was brought in with a compound fracture of the leg (a fracture is compound when the skin is broken by a piece of the bone). He treated the wound with a carbolic solution. It was useless; the man died and Lister tried to console himself with the thought that the man had been in such a bad condition that he would have died in any case. It was four months before he dared to try it again. This time it was on a boy of twelve who had an open wound on his leg. He treated it carefully and waited in great anxiety for the result. On the fourth day the boy said his leg hurt. Lister was in despair. Was this too going to be a failure? He removed the dressing and found the wound was healing perfectly; the pain had only come because the carbolic was too strong and had burned the skin. After several more successes with this method of getting rid of germs, Lister addressed meetings on the subject but was met with scepticism from most of his hearers. Florence Nightingale was scornful. 'Germs,' she said, 'I've never seen them.'

Above: A carbolic spray used by Lister in his operating theatre.

Below: An operation under antiseptic conditions, using a carbolic spray and chloroform inhaler.

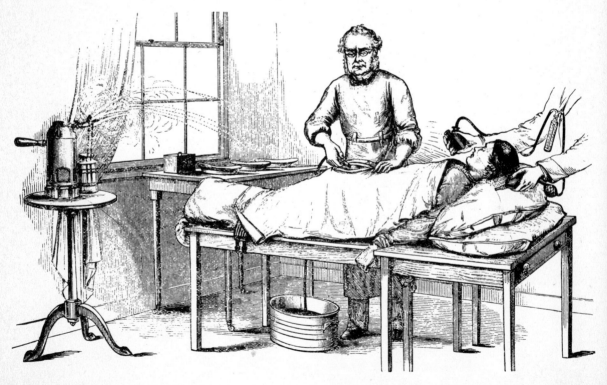

A men's ward in 1860. Visitors are allowed and there are curtains round the beds. Potted plants and birdcages show that efforts are being made to make the ward more pleasant.

On Professor Syme's death Lister was given the post of Professor of Surgery in Edinburgh and built round himself a school of young surgeons trained in this antiseptic technique. Now he could claim that not 50 per cent, but 97 per cent of his patients lived. Other doctors were still critical, but the citizens of Edinburgh obstinately preferred to live rather than die after an operation, and in that city he was held in high honour. Later he came to London to work at King's College Hospital, and the success of his work at last convinced the London surgeons of its value.

Great advances are seldom made by one man alone. A body of knowledge is slowly built up and then one man may find the missing key to what has puzzled the scientists. Pasteur had discovered germs; Lister found out that germs were a cause of putrefaction and invented methods of killing them.

In 1892 a celebration was held in Paris in honour of Pasteur's seventieth birthday. It was presided over by the President of the French Republic. Ambassadors, men of science, dignitaries of all kinds were there. Lister was brought on the platform to bring greetings from the Royal Society of Edinburgh and the Royal Society of London. In a short speech he said that Pasteur had 'raised the veil which for centuries had covered infectious disease.'

We can see what an enormous advance was made during the nineteenth century. There were still many obstinate diseases for which no

cure had been found, but the work of Pasteur had shown how to attack the problem. This is not of course to say that all disease is caused by germs, but in the battle against sickness doctors now had the help of chemists and physicists, and were no longer fumbling in the dark. If we want to see the practical results of this we only have to look at the tables showing the fever mortality rate.

Lister (on the platform) addressing Pasteur in Paris, on Pasteur's seventieth birthday in 1892.
The celebration marked the formal recognition of the important advances made in medicine.

Dates to remember

1846 An anaesthetic used for the first time in England
1860 Florence Nightingale School for Nurses opened at St Thomas's Hospital

Things to do

1 Find out all you can about your local hospital, that is who founded it and when. It would be interesting to make your own history of the hospital, how big the wards were, how many patients did the hospital take in, what were the nurses paid. You may be able to get this information from your library.
2 Find out if there was ever a fever hospital in your neighbourhood and what it is used for now.

St Thomas's Hospital, where Florence Nightingale founded her school of nursing. It was her idea that the hospital should be designed in separate blocks to admit more light and air.

3　How is Pasteur associated with the milk we drink?
4　What serious diseases have we not yet conquered?
5　Read the lives of some of the men who made important medical discoveries, and think what qualities they had which led to their success.

Books to read

M. J. Burton, *Louis Pasteur*, Chatto & Windus
Ritchie Calder, *Medicine and Man*, Allen & Unwin
F. F. Cartwright, *Joseph Lister*, Weidenfeld & Nicolson
P. Chambers, *Great Company – fight against disease*, Bodley Head
J. Rowland, *The Chloroform Man*, Lutterworth
Boswell Taylor, *Medicine*, Ward Lock Educational
N. Wymer, *Medical Scientists and Doctors*, Oxford University Press

Chapter 12
The British Empire

Britain was a rich and powerful country, partly because of her Empire.

Look at the map of the world in 1878 below and notice all the parts which are shaded. Those places belonged to Britain. You will see a large area in North America, the whole of Australia and New Zealand, India, parts of Africa, and numbers of little islands from the West Indies, right round to Hongkong off the coast of China.

What made the English people leave their homes and wander all over the globe? How could so small an island manage to conquer and control all that territory? The chief reason was our wealth after the industrial revolution, which enabled us to keep the most powerful fleet in the world. This fleet protected our traders and made it possible for us to take possession of new lands.

Canada

Men started to go westward in the seventeenth century. If a farmer had four sons one of them might inherit the farm. What about the other

The British Empire in 1878.

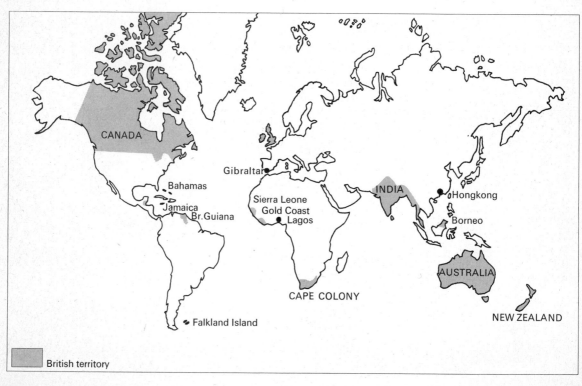

British territory

three? Some of the most enterprising went to the east coast of America where land could be had for the asking. Later, after these first colonies became independent of Britain, another place had to be found where land was free or cheap. North of these original colonies lay Canada; the eastern part of it, round Quebec, was occupied by French people whom we had conquered in the Seven Years' War, but farther west, Upper Canada or Ontario as it was called, had vast unclaimed forests. If we hear nowadays of friends going to Canada, we do not think of it as a great adventure. We know that they will have a short and comfortable journey whether by sea or air, that they will probably already have friends or relations there. They are going to a country where there are towns, railways, airways and all the comforts of civilization.

What was it like to go to Canada in the 1820s? First of all the journey was made in a sailing ship; it lasted sometimes as long as ten weeks, and they were not very comfortable weeks. Then, when the settlers arrived, they did not find a home ready made, no welcoming friends to greet them. Some of those who went were not willing exiles, they would rather have stayed in their homes. They went because they were turned out of their homes in Britain. The most famous of these evictions were those of Sutherland in the very north of Scotland. The landlords in the Highlands of Scotland in the early nineteenth century found they could make more money by running sheep over the hills than by accepting small rents from their tenants. The woollen industry was booming,

Living-quarters on a ship used for carrying distressed gentle-women to Canada in 1850.

and there was a great demand for wool. The crofters of Sutherland, the old and the sick as well as the young and strong, were driven from their homes, and to ensure that they did not come back, the homes were burned down. Numbers of them sailed to Canada. Here is a description of their journey, written by one of them:

The old and the children could not stand the hardships of the voyage, every day one or more of our group was buried at sea. After tossing on the Atlantic for eleven weeks we came to the coast of Canada. Each day we had to pay for our food and as some of us had a little money left, the Captain of the vessel cruised up and down for three weeks before he landed us, penniless on the Canadian shore. We were taken by bullock waggon to Toronto. There we stayed in sheds put up for the emigrants. Smallpox was raging and carried off many who had survived the voyage. Then we were given an Indian guide, a sack of maize-meal, a sack of seed potatoes and a plough. We marched a hundred miles and were left in the middle of a forest to make our homes. We had to burn down the trees before we could plant the potatoes. For six months we had nothing to eat but maize-meal and water.

It was by the hard slogging work of tough pioneers like this that Canada was built.

Of course, when roads were made and when railways were built conditions became easier. Emigrants then went farther west to the great prairies where for miles and miles, as far as the eye could see, there was rolling grassy country without a single tree. Here wheat was grown and dispatched by rail and sea to England. Farther west still there were cattle ranches. Canada became a chief supplier of food to Great Britain.

A Canadian farm fifteen years after settlement.

Indians hunting bison in the 1830s. Later these prairies became the wheat and cattle lands of central Canada.

In 1867 all the different provinces joined together to form the 'Dominion of Canada'. The last barrier against settlement in West Canada was crossed when the railway was extended over the Rocky Mountains to British Columbia on the Pacific coast, and that province was joined to the dominion. The capital of the country was named Ottawa. The Canadians had their own Parliament and made their own laws. The government at home did not interfere with them as it had done with the earlier American colonies.

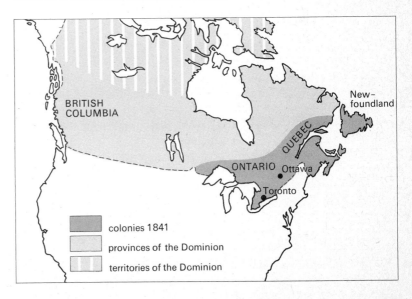

Map of Canada.

Australia and New Zealand

'Australia became prosperous because of the wickedness of England,' someone said. What was meant by this? Simply that in the beginning Australia was a place to which convicts were sent. It was expensive to keep them in prison and the government was anxious to be rid of them. Before 1783 we had shipped convicts to the American colonies, where they worked out their sentence under a master who employed them. But the United States of America after 1783 did not want any more of these unruly immigrants. For a year or two they were kept in disused rotting ships on the Thames, until the suggestion was made that Australia, 12,000 miles away, would be an excellent country to harbour them. Captain Cook had sailed round the coast and discovered a place he called Botany Bay because the flowers there were so wonderful, and this was chosen for a convict settlement.

A certain Captain Phillip was given charge of the first group to go there in 1788. After five months' sailing they arrived at Botany Bay, but Captain Phillip decided it was not suitable and went farther on and landed at what is now called Sydney Harbour. The term Botany Bay was nevertheless used for this colony. In a children's game right up to the present century there was a rhyme:

Here comes an old woman from Botany Bay
What have you got to give her today?

Botany Bay.

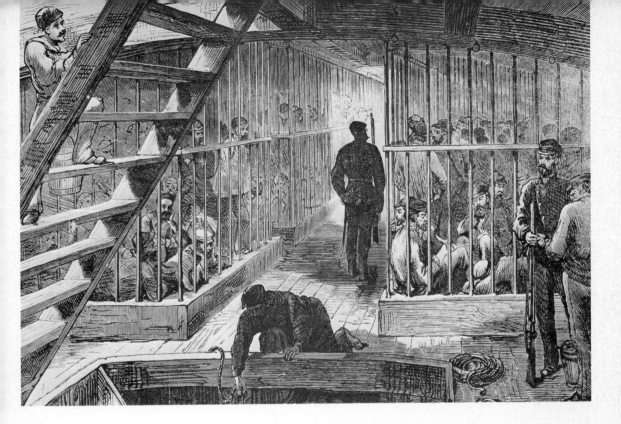

Transport ship carrying convicts.

The government had shown little imagination in beginning this venture. Captain Phillip begged for more supplies. He needed seeds, farm implements, and food. Instead he was sent more convicts. The food ran short and was strictly rationed. Then it was stolen and guards were put on it. But the soldiers who were there to guard the convicts were as dishonest and thievish as the men they had to look after. Captain Phillip had to deal with a mixed group; some of them might be desperate criminals, others men who had perhaps snared a rabbit or stolen a loaf of bread. When the laws in England were harsh, all sorts and conditions of men were transported, some of them simply because the government of the day did not like their opinions. After four years of unrewarding labour Captain Phillip retired because of ill-health.

For the convicts it was often a hard and brutal life. They were at the mercy of officers who could be cruel and vindictive. Justice – such as it was – was 12,000 miles away. If an officer had a reliable servant he could keep him long after his sentence was finished. Some of the convicts escaped into the bush and became 'bush rangers', a terror to everyone. They were desperate men and knew what their fate would be if they were caught; they would be sent to the dreaded Norfolk Island, a place of horrors kept for the worst offenders. So they would not hesitate to murder anyone who might find them and give them away.

There was another side to the picture. The children who were born there had a better chance than if they were reared in an English slum.

Left: Shearing sheep by hand.

The first generation of children grew so tall and healthy they were nicknamed the 'cornstalks'.

Some of these convicts later on became prosperous and made a name for themselves. Mary Reibey, a little English girl of thirteen, lived with her grandmother in the country. She was high-spirited and mischievous. One day she saw a pony grazing in a field; she ran into the field, captured the pony and rode round on it for a few minutes. For this crime she was transported. After a hard beginning, she finished her sentence and married a businessman in the colony. On his death she carried on his shipping business, but she did not forget what it was like to be carried away from home to a faraway country. She ran a home for the girls, who, like herself, had been transported. She looked after their interest and became one of the most respected women in Australia.

A change came to the colony with the introduction of sheep. One of the officers brought in eight merino sheep in 1789; a hundred years later the number in the country was 106,000,000. They prospered on the grassy lands and the manufacturers in Yorkshire found the Australian wool was of excellent quality. When this fact became known there was a rush of fortune-hunters from England, who got 'sheep stations' as they were called, and employed convict labour. Soon these free settlers outnumbered the convicts. Australia became an attractive place. Dickens, at the end of his novel *David Copperfield*, when he has a lot of characters to dispose of, sends them, Micawbers and all, to Australia. In real life, he sent out two of his sons to work there. Many of the ex-convicts grew rich, like Magwitch in *Great Expectations*. After a time the free settlers wished Australia to be respectable, and objected to the system of transportation. By 1852 it stopped completely.

The interior of Australia was hot and dry, but round the coast there was good farming land, and other towns were founded: Melbourne, Adelaide, and Brisbane. Gold was discovered near Melbourne, and that brought emigrants from all over the world. Australia, like Canada, supplied Great Britain with food. The different provinces united in

Below: Washing for gold in New South Wales, 1852. The gold dust was supposed to sink to the bottom.

A New Zealand Maori war canoe.

1900, and took the name of the Commonwealth of Australia, making their capital at Canberra.

New Zealand was colonized later than Australia, and like that country found that sheep-rearing was profitable. After the invention of refrigeration, meat as well as wool was sent to Great Britain.

These three colonies, though they admitted emigrants from other countries, developed along English lines. The people who went there took with them the English language, English law and English customs. They had to adapt themselves to a different climate and had to discover different methods of farming, but they were a part of Great Britain which had transplanted itself across the sea.

Who held the land before the Europeans came?

We speak of men settling in these countries as if they had before that been uninhabited. But in fact all of them, although sparsely populated, had native peoples there. In Canada there were wandering tribes of

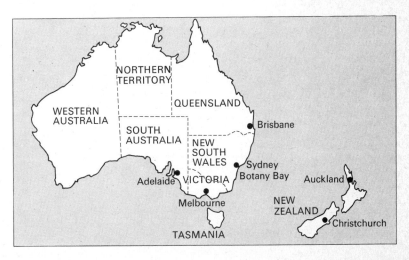

Right: Map of Australia and New Zealand.

Left: A poster issued in 1816 by the governor of Tasmania to the native inhabitants. The top two sections promise friendship between the races. The two lower sections declare that a single code of law will apply to all law-breakers, white or black. However, by 1876 there were no blacks in Tasmania: they had been killed off.

Indians who resented the coming of the white man, because he took the land and cut down the forests where they had hunted. There was no room for both the hunting Indian and the white farmer, so the Indians were pushed farther north and finally were given 'reservations'; these are areas which are reserved for them. In Australia the native races had been cut off by distance from other civilizations and had not advanced beyond the Stone Age level. The invaders called them simply 'the Blacks' and treated them like animals. They shot them as they would have shot game. So the poor Blacks moved away from the coastal regions where they had lived and went into the interior of the country, leaving their old home to the Englishman. In New Zealand the colonists met a much more highly-developed race, the Maoris. Against them fierce wars were fought. Peace only came when the Maoris accepted defeat and a division of the land, which left some of it to the original inhabitants.

A state procession in India in the late eighteenth century.

India

It is easy to understand why Englishmen who wanted land should seek their fortune abroad. But why should they go to the Far East, to India, which was a thickly populated country, and had a climate hard for Europeans to endure? The answer is, they did not go there to live, they went there to trade. India was not to become a permanent home, like Canada or Australia. It was a land in which money could be made.

England was an island with splendid natural harbours and an abundant supply of wood for making ships. Ever since the Middle Ages trading companies had carried goods abroad, to the Baltic and to the Mediterranean. The most precious goods came from the East. These had to be brought over land to the Mediterranean and then by sea to Britain. When the route round the Cape of Good Hope was discovered it became possible to go all the way to the East by sea. The East India Company (founded 1600) began to make regular voyages there; so did the Dutch, the French and the Portuguese. The first thing the Company had to do was to get permission from the local rulers to set up trading stations. We soon had three of these, in Calcutta, Bombay and Madras. And using these three as bases the Company gradually got control of a good part of India. A trading company could not have got so much power if India had been united and well governed. It was neither. It was a feudal country split up into numbers of different states, ruled over by the Great Mogul who lived in Delhi. Once these states had formed a mighty, cultured, oriental empire, but by the seventeenth century the power of the Great Mogul had declined, and decay had set in. The East India Company cleverly took advantage of quarrels between the states. They kept a small army, equipped with European weapons, to defend their trading stations, and they could offer the services of this army to the princes in return for possibly a slice of territory, or else for the privilege of collecting the taxes and controlling the currency. The Company found that it was easier to trade with a country in which it had political power. The Company could build roads where it wanted them, go into the interior, and make good terms for its traders.

East India, policy of the Company

The Company was careful to treat the princes handsomely. If they took over the government of one of the provinces they gave the Prince a generous pension and promised to protect him from his enemies. Many of the princes thought it better to be on good terms with the Company than to fight it. In the first years of its existence possibly only one ship a year would be sent to India. By the eighteenth century many ships would sail every year into the East India Docks in London, laden with tea, spices, muslins, carpets and silks. In 1784 the British government decided to take some control over the Company. They appointed a Governor-General who had authority over the conduct of affairs. A regular army was raised with Indian soldiers (called Sepoys) commanded by British officers. During the Napoleonic wars the French attacked the British in India, but failed to dislodge them. If you look at the map you will see that by 1805 a great deal of India was in British hands.

What sort of men chose to go out to India to work for the Company? They were those who were attracted by the romance of the East and by the glittering prizes they might gain. There was little real information about that country. They had heard that the rajahs (as the princes were called) were fabulously rich, that their clothes were studded with pearls and rubies, and that they rode on bejewelled elephants. They went out there – a long voyage of five months – to work until they had made a fortune and could retire to England. Many of them did come home rich. Many of them never came home at all. They had to face a hot climate, and diseases unknown in the West, from which the chance of recovery was slight. If they survived they had rewards. For some trifling service to a rajah they might be given a handsome amount of money or some fabulous jewels. It was difficult to draw the line between

An Indian sculpture of Buddha, the great religious teacher. It dates from the second or third century A.D.

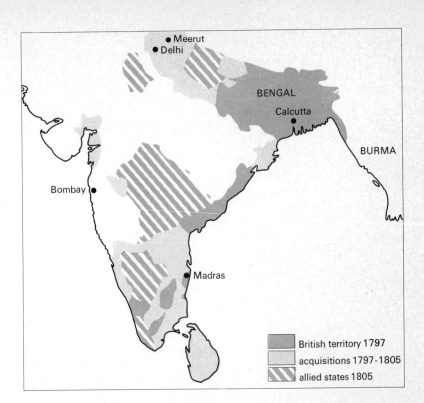

British possessions in India up to 1805.

accepting a present and taking a bribe. Only when the Company was forced to pay higher salaries to its servants was it possible to stop corruption. Service in the company provided openings for middle-class people. The grandfather of the novelist Thackeray had nine sons and he sent them all to India. Many of those East India officers worked hard and conscientiously and genuinely wanted to do the best for the Indian people. But they could not help thinking that English ways were the right ones. They thought it their duty to train the Indians to be like the British, and the schools and colleges which were set up gave all their instruction in the English language. Therefore if an Indian wanted to get on in life, he must learn English. Often English officials failed to understand the Indian traditions, and because of this ignorance, and not through ill-will, would give a wrong decision in the court of law. The Indians were far behind the British in all technical things, and therefore the officials assumed they were behind in every-thing. Very few of them studied the history of India or read any of her books.

Lord Dalhousie and his policy

One of the governor-generals, Lord Dalhousie, was particularly enraged by what he thought was Indian inefficiency. He sincerely thought that by far the best thing for the Indians was for Great Britain to have control over the whole of India. On one occasion he seized a wealthy province by means which the Indians thought unjust. He wanted India to be up to date and saw no chance of this happening under the old-fashioned rule of the rajahs. He began the building of the Great Trunk Road from Calcutta to Amritsar. Railways were built and a postal and telegraph system established. When he left at the end of his term of service he did not realize the resentment he had caused.

The caste system was deeply rooted in Indian tradition. In the railways high and low caste had to mix. A law was passed taking away from prisoners the right to cook their own food while in jail. It might be cooked by outcasts and therefore, according to Hindu ideas, it was polluted. Rumours were spread that the Sepoys were to be taken across the water to fight in Burma, and a Hindu broke the laws of his caste if he travelled over the sea. Then new Lee Enfield rifles were given to the troops. The grease which covered the cartridges had to be bitten off. The soldiers believed the grease was made from the fat of pigs and cows. The pig was unclean to the Mohammedans and the cow was sacred to the Hindus. It was tragic that the officers did not take the objection to the new rifle seriously. They dismissed it as stupid oriental prejudice. In 1757, a hundred years before, Clive had won a great victory at Plassey, which had established our rule in Bengal. Indians remembered the prophecy that British power in India would only last a hundred years.

The Mutiny 1857–8

Soon after Dalhousie returned home, in 1857, frightening news burst on the people in Britain. There had been a mutiny of the Sepoys in Northern India. Thousands of English families had relations or friends there and they were frantic with anxiety. The Mutiny was confined to a small part of the north of India and centred on Delhi, where the Great Mogul was brought out of his palace and restored to his throne. It would have been far more dangerous for the British if the Mutiny had been carefully organized beforehand, or if the whole of India had joined in. But even as things were, it was nearly a year before the revolt was over. Both sides behaved with terrible cruelty, and for the same reason – fear. The British had few troops in India at that time; they had been drawn away to fight in the Crimean War, and there was – or so it seemed at the time – a possibility that the British community could be completely wiped out. The Sepoys too knew that they would meet a terrible fate if they lost the struggle and were taken captive. Both sides fought with the courage of desperation. They did not stop to find out whether their victims were guilty or not. It was kill or be killed. After it was over the East India Company was abolished and the British government took over complete control.

The Mutiny had been a great shock to the British people. The government ordered that more British troops should be stationed in India, and they saw to it that the religious ideas and prejudices of the Indians should be respected.

Destruction of a bungalow at Meerut at the beginning of the Mutiny. Civilians, including women and children, were killed indiscriminately.

The Mutiny put an end to the possibility of happy or friendly relations between the races. Both sides had bitter memories and suspicions. The British kept to themselves, and though the officials had to meet the Indians in the course of their duties, they did not mix with them socially. Many young Indians came to England to study and were impressed by what they saw in the West and realized how backward their country was in some ways. In 1885 a movement started called the Indian Congress; young men from all parts of India met each year to discuss the problems of their country. They admired what the British had achieved, and wanted to learn from them; at the same time they did not want to be ruled by a foreign power, and worked for Indian independence. The British government always declared that they would only stay in India until the Indians had learned to rule themselves, and gradually more responsibility was given to the people of the country. But many Indians began to think that they were waiting too long and became impatient for the time when the British would leave.

Left: This bronze from Benin shows a highly sophisticated technique in metal work.

Africa – 'The dark continent'

What do the words 'tropical Africa' suggest to you? Do you think of dense forests, of elephants and lions, and other wild animals? We now know a great deal about Africa, but until the middle of the nineteenth century Europeans were quite ignorant of what the centre of this vast continent was like. To most people it was a huge jungle inhabited by savage tribes, and they knew that somewhere near the equator there were the mysterious mountains where the Nile had its source. Recently archaeologists have discovered remains of what must have been prosperous and orderly kingdoms, and this account, written by a Dutch traveller in 1700, describes what these kingdoms may have been like before they were broken up by slave-raiding wars:

Benin 1700

The inhabitants of this Country, if possessed of any riches, eat and drink well; that is to say, of the best. The common diet of the rich is Beef, Mutton or Chickens, and Jammes (yams) for the Bread; which, after they have boiled, they beat very fine, in order to make cakes of it; they frequently treat one another, and impart a portion of their superfluity to the necessitous.

The meaner sort content themselves with smoked or dried Fish, which, if salted, is very like what we in Europe call Raf or Reekel; their Bread is also Jammes, Bananas, and Beans; their drink, Water and Pardon-Wine, which is none of the best. The meaner sort drink Water, Brandy when they can get it. The King, the great Lords, and every Governor who is but indifferently rich, subsist several Poor at their Place of Residence on their Charity, employing those who are fit for any work, in order to help them to a Maintenance, and the rest they keep for God's sake, and to obtain the Character of being charitable; so there are no Beggars: and this necessary care succeeds so well that we do not see many remarkably poor amongst them. . . .

The King has a very rich Income; for his Territories are very large and full of Governors, and each knows how many Bags of Boesies (cowries), the Money of this Country, he must annually raise to the King, which amounts to a vast Sum, which 'tis impossible to make any Calculation of. Others, of a meaner Rank than the former, instead of Money, deliver to the King Bulls, Cows, Sheep, Chickens, Jammes and Cloathes; in short, whatever he wants to his Housekeeping. . . .

Our first connexion with the west coast of Africa was the shameful one of the slave-trade. After this was abolished the traders found other kinds of desirable goods, ivory, ebony, gold and palm-oil. Many European traders lost their lives on this fever-haunted coast, which was nick-named 'the white man's grave'. An old sailors' rhyme runs:

Take care and beware of the Bight of Benin,
Here two come out where forty went in.

Mary Kingsley, a bold woman traveller of the time of Queen Victoria, has described the coast at the mouth of Bonny River:

. . . come inside the bar, and anchor off the factories: seaward there is the foam of the bar, gleaming and wicked – white against a leaden sky, and what is left of Breaker Island. In every other direction you will see the apparently endless walls of mangrove, unvarying in colour, unvarying in form, unvarying in height. . . . Beneath and between you and them lie the rotting mud waters of Bonny River, and away up and down river miles of rotting mud mangrove swamp. The only break in them and one can hardly call it a relief to the scenery, are the gaunt black ribs of the old hulks, once used as trading stations, which lie exposed at low water near the shore, protruding like the skeletons of great, unclean beasts who have died because Bonny water was too strong even for them.

Raised on piles from the mud shore you will see the white-painted factories and their store houses for oil, each factory likely enough with its flag at half-mast, which does not enliven the scenery either, for you know it is because somebody is 'dead again'. Throughout and overall is the torrential down-pour of the wet season rain, coming down night and day with its dull roar. I have known it rain for six weeks at Bonny River. It is near evening time now, you can watch the mist becoming incarnate, creeping and

Above: Bronze head from Nigeria, probably of the thirteenth or fourteenth century A.D.

crawling and gliding out from the side creeks and between the mangrove roots, laying itself upon the river, stretching and rolling in a kind of grim play, and finally, crawling up the side of the ship to come on board and leave its cloak of moisture that grows green mildew in a few hours over all.

Other countries besides Britain found the trade of the tropical coast profitable. Portugal had had colonies in Africa since the sixteenth century, and so had Spain. France and Germany began to cast covetous eyes on Central Africa. In 1884 all the chief European powers met to carve up Africa amongst themselves.

Britain's share on the west coast was Ghana, which was then called the Gold Coast, and Nigeria, our largest and most profitable African colony. On the east coast we obtained Kenya and Uganda. Look at the map and see how the different parts of Africa were handed over to European rulers.

The European countries sent out explorers far into the interior to

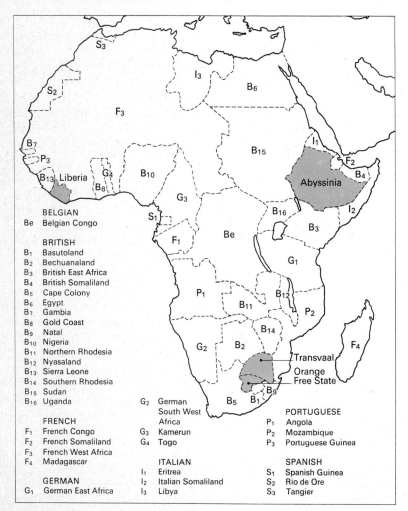

BELGIAN
Be Belgian Congo

BRITISH
B₁ Basutoland
B₂ Bechuanaland
B₃ British East Africa
B₄ British Somaliland
B₅ Cape Colony
B₆ Egypt
B₇ Gambia
B₈ Gold Coast
B₉ Natal
B₁₀ Nigeria
B₁₁ Northern Rhodesia
B₁₂ Nyasaland
B₁₃ Sierra Leone
B₁₄ Southern Rhodesia
B₁₅ Sudan
B₁₆ Uganda

FRENCH
F₁ French Congo
F₂ French Somaliland
F₃ French West Africa
F₄ Madagascar

GERMAN
G₁ German East Africa

G₂ German South West Africa
G₃ Kamerun
G₄ Togo

ITALIAN
I₁ Eritrea
I₂ Italian Somaliland
I₃ Libya

PORTUGUESE
P₁ Angola
P₂ Mozambique
P₃ Portuguese Guinea

SPANISH
S₁ Spanish Guinea
S₂ Rio de Ore
S₃ Tangier

The division of Africa began in 1884 and continued into the twentieth century. The grey areas mark the only independent states. Transvaal and the Orange Free State became British in 1902.

David Livingstone carried by his faithful servant, Susi.

David Livingstone.

find out about their new possessions. One of the most remarkable of these men was David Livingstone, who went out, not as an explorer, but as a medical missionary. His work led him into the heart of Africa. He was horrified when he saw how the Arab slavers were raiding the villages and carrying off the Africans. He sent back accurate reports to England, not only of the slave-trade, but also of the country itself. He helped to chart the great unknown wilderness of the continent. He had a scientific interest in all that he saw. Hardship and discomfort seemed nothing to him as he pushed his way through difficult jungle country.

He started the last of his great journeys when he was fifty-two, in 1865. By this time his explorations and discoveries had made him famous and the Royal Geographical Society equipped this expedition. For nearly five years nothing was heard of him. Then an American journalist, Stanley, set out to follow in his tracks and found Livingstone ill and exhausted. Some of his helpers had died and his medical supplies had been lost. Stanley gave him the supplies he had brought with him and then returned to Zanzibar, taking with him Livingstone's diary. He promised to send him some porters to help him to continue his journey. When the porters arrived Livingstone started again on his quest. After some months his strength gave out and he had to be carried in a litter. In May 1873 he died. His two faithful boys, Susi and Chuma, wrapped his body in a cloth and put it in a cylinder of bark. They carried it down a thousand miles to Zanzibar. Not only was this journey long and difficult, it was also dangerous. Perhaps this action more than anything else shows how the Africans loved and reverenced Livingstone.

The Africans lost their independence when the Europeans conquered and occupied their countries, but they gained in many ways. The Europeans built railways so that goods could be brought to the harbours, and along these railways, and along the great rivers where the trading boats went, new ideas and new techniques began to develop. It was found that jungle paths could be made into easy, shady bicycle tracks, and soon a bicycle became the most treasured possession of a prosperous African. Even the governor and his wife travelled by bicycle in the early days; colonial civil servants could not then live comfortable lives in offices. Most important, missionaries built hospitals and schools; central Africa began to move into the modern world.

The Africans were backward, but they were not therefore inferior to Europeans. There is a great deal of difference in the meaning of these two words. A child who has been prevented from going to school for some time may well be backward, but if he is given a chance to make up for lost time he can do it. He is not inferior; it is merely that he has not had the same chance as other children.

The Africans were expert in some kinds of weaving and metal work, but they knew nothing of machinery. One reason for this is the tremendous odds against which they had had to fight. For instance, there is the difficulty of farming in a country where in large areas cattle cannot be kept for meat, milk, or pulling ploughs, because of tsetse fly, and the tropical forest prevents the growing of grain. Also Africans suffer from the weakening diseases, malaria and dysentery.

Africans began in the nineteenth century to make rapid progress and some who had begun their education in mission schools went to Great Britain for more advanced studies.

North and South Africa

What about the northern and southern parts of Africa? In the north, England obtained partial control of Egypt, and also owned half the shares of the Suez Canal Company; the other half was owned by France. Britain laid great importance on having some authority in Egypt because the shortest route to India lay through the Canal.

In the southern part of Africa, thousands of miles from Egypt, Britain bought Cape Colony from the Dutch in 1815. This was a healthy beautiful country in which white people flourished. Holland had sent settlers there in the seventeenth century, and French Huguenot refugees had also gone there. The early settlers met a tall, strong race of Africans, the Bantu people. Because the Europeans had firearms they conquered the Bantu, took their lands and made them servants, as we have explained in Chapter 3. When in 1833 slavery was abolished in the British Empire, the Dutch farmers (who were called Boers) were aggrieved. They did not think the compensation which they were paid for the loss of their slaves was enough. So some of them in 1836 undertook what was called 'The Great Trek'. They wandered northwards in covered wagons with their families, their household goods and their cattle, until they came to a part of the country beyond the Orange River and the Vaal River; they stayed there and called it Transvaal. Later some of them settled in the Orange Free State.

Now look at the map showing the positions of the British and the

Above: Zulu warrior. An illustration from a book of the 1850s.

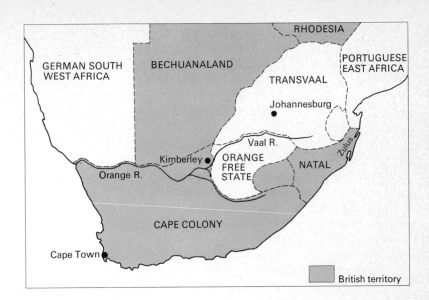

South Africa at the outbreak of the Boer War in 1899.

Below: Photographs of Cape Town with Table Mountain in the background, from an album published in 1866.

Boers. The British had taken another colony called Natal, and the Boers were without any direct route to the coast. They had to cross over Portuguese territory to get to the sea. They had to protect themselves against attacks by the Zulus, who resented their land being taken. The Boers called on Britain to help them fight the Zulus.

These four colonies, two British and two Boer, might have had a different history, if one morning a little boy had not shown his father a bright stone he had picked up on the farm. The stone was a diamond. Immediately there was a rush to Kimberley where the diamond fields were found. Among those who came out to South Africa was a young man called Cecil Rhodes. He came because of ill-health. He made a fortune in the diamond mining industry. Then gold was discovered at Johannesburg, and Rhodes made another fortune in gold, so that his

income was estimated at £2,000,000 a year. He became Prime Minister of Cape Colony. He laid ambitious plans. At first he thought of combining with the Boers and forming a sort of federation of African states all under the British flag. He got the permission of the British government to found a trading company to explore north of Cape Colony. He made treaties of friendship with the chiefs and took over Bechuanaland which then became a British protectorate. It is often said that Rhodes was skilful in dealing with the African chiefs, and was liked by them. He was certainly skilful in cheating them, and they found too late what the treaties they were persuaded to sign really meant.

Lobengula signed with his mark a treaty which gave away the right to his land and the minerals under it in return for a few guns and some trifling luxuries; he thought that he was merely giving the Europeans the right to graze animals and camp in his territories.

Rhodes went north from Bechuanaland and that part was named after him, Rhodesia. Finally he wanted to build a railway from Cape Town to Cairo. As the Americans would say, 'He thought big.'

In the meantime all was not well in the Transvaal. Johannesburg was full of go-getters, scum from all over the world, who had come to get rich quick on gold. The Boer government taxed them heavily and would not allow them to become citizens, so that they could not vote. When they complained, the answer of old President Kruger was 'If you don't like our country, you can go.'

Rhodes wanted to get the Transvaal under his control, so that he could make a British route right through Africa, from Cape Town to Cairo; he hoped that the Uitlanders (as the foreigners in the Transvaal were called) could be persuaded to rebel against Kruger and set up a pro-British government. In an evil moment for him he agreed to a plan by which his friend, Captain Jameson, was to send a small force of cavalry to Johannesburg; he thought that the Uitlanders would rise up and welcome them and that they would force Kruger to yield to their demands.

The raid failed miserably. The Uitlanders did not rise. Rhodes was disgraced for having planned to overthrow the government of a neighbouring country, and had to give up his position as Prime Minister of Cape Colony. Kruger now knew that Britain was his enemy, and he accordingly made preparations for war by buying arms and ammunition from Germany.

Finally, in 1899, war broke out between Great Britain and the Transvaal.

The mighty British Empire was at war with 50,000 farmers. It would be over in a month, people thought. Actually it lasted nearly three years, and the rest of the world laughed to see Great Britain in difficulties. English people travelling abroad were mocked by calls of 'The Boers are coming.' Why did the war last so long? The Boers fought in an unexpected way, which was that all of them fought. They would look after their farms by day, go out at night on a Commando raid,

Above right: The Boers manning their trenches outside Mafeking. They besieged the town from October 1899 to May 1900.

Below right: Hampstead celebrating the relief of Mafeking. 'B.P.' on the banner stands for Baden-Powell, whose picture is being carried. His defence of Mafeking made him a national hero.

and then return to their farms. They were excellent marksmen and horsemen. They were fighting in their own country. The British army command took a long time to deal with the situation, and they only won finally when they took the women and children and kept them in camps, and destroyed the farms.

The Boers have not yet forgotten these camps; they were badly run, typhoid broke out in them and thousands of the inmates died.

When peace was made in 1902, the two Boer republics became British.

The end of Victoria's reign

By the end of the nineteenth century the European nations seemed to have conquered the world. America had been colonized from Europe. Australia, New Zealand, all Africa, except Abyssinia and Sierra Leone and Liberia, belonged to European countries. Most of India was British; China, though independent, had been marked out on the maps with spheres of influence for Britain, France and Germany. What would happen now that the underdeveloped countries had been colonized? Would the Europeans have to conquer the moon or would they fight each other?

Queen Victoria died in 1901, before the end of the Boer War. Most English people could not remember the time when she was not on the throne. When the newspapers appeared with deep black borders announcing her death, it seemed as if an end had come to something which had been secure. She had reigned for nearly sixty-four years, longer than any other British sovereign, and had seen her country grow into the most powerful nation in the world governing an empire 'on which the sun never set.'

Dates to remember

1857–8	Indian Mutiny
1867	Dominion of Canada founded
1899–1902	Boer War
1900	Commonwealth of Australia founded

Things to do

1 Make a list of foodstuffs and raw materials which we get from each colony.
2 Make a list of words which have come into the English language from South Africa, India and Malaya.
3 All the education provided in India was given in the English language. Discuss whether this was an advantage or a disadvantage for the Indians.
4 Make a list of the French and Portuguese colonies of the nineteenth century.

Interesting people to read about: Macquarie, Lord Durham, Gibbon Wakefield, Lord John Lawrence, Cecil Rhodes, Kipling.

Books to read

Colin Clive, *Mary Kingsley*, Bruce & Gawthorne
Colin Clive, *Lachlan Macquarie*, Bruce & Gawthorne
R. Collier, *The Sound of Fury*, Collins
A. Williams-Ellis, *Changing the World*, Bodley Head
Basil Matthews, *Livingstone*, Black
Alan Moorehead, *The White Nile*, Penguin
Margaret Murray, *My first Hundred Years*, Kimber
C. Turnbull, *Concise History of Australia*, Thames & Hudson

Early stamps from Australia, Canada, India and the Cape of Good Hope.

Index

Numbers listed in italics (e.g. *15*) refer to the captions of illustrations and maps.

Act of Union (1800), 127
  see also Ireland
Adelaide, *see* Australia
Africa, 208–16
  Bantus, 212
  Benin, 208–9, *208*
  Bonny River, 209–10
  Cape Colony, 212
  Cape Town, *213*
  colonizers in, 210
  diamonds, 213
  Ghana, 210
  gold, 213
  Kenya, 210
  Kimberley, 213
  Natal, 213
  Nigeria, *209*, 210
  Rhodesia, 214
  stamps, *217*
  Transvaal, 47, 212, 214
  Zulus, *212*, 213
  see also Boers
Albert, Prince, of Saxe-Coburg-
  Gotha (1819–61),
  averts war with America, 82
  death, 83
  marries Queen Victoria, 62
  organizes Great Exhibition,
  96–8
Alexander I, Emperor of Russia
  (1777–1825), 21, 28
Alma, Battle of the (1854), *78*
  see also Crimean War
Amalgamated Society of Engineers,
  113
American Civil War (1861–5), 82
  Alabama incident, 105
Amiens, Peace of (1802), 19
Anaesthetics, 187–8, *188–90*
  see also Medicine
Anti-Corn Law League, 68
  see also Corn Laws
Anti-Vaccine Society, *182*
  see also Medicine
Arabi Pasha (1841?–1911), 109–10

Architecture, Victorian, 140–2,
  141, 142
Arrow, Chinese ship, 81–2
Attwood, Thomas (1783–1856), 40
Austen, Jane (1775–1817), 60
Austerlitz, Battle of (1805), 21
  see also Bonaparte, Napoleon
Australia, 198–201
  Aborigines ('the Blacks'), 202
  Botany Bay, 198, *198*
  convicts, *199*, 199–200
  sheep-shearing, *200*
  stamp, *217*
  washing for gold in, *200*
Austria, at war with France
  (1792–5), 9–11, (1805), 20

Balaclava, 76–7, *76*
  Charge of the Light Brigade, *79*
  see also Crimean War
Balfour, Arthur James, Earl of
  (1848–1930), 132
Bank holidays, 95
Bantus, *see* Africa
Barnardo, Dr Thomas (1845–1905),
  116
Bastille, *7, 8*
Beagle, 160
Bell, Alexander Graham (1847–
  1922), 167
Benefit clubs, 113, *113*
Benin, 208–9, *208*
Beresina River, Russia, 23, *23*
Berlin Decrees, 21–2
  see also Bonaparte, Napoleon
Berlin, Treaty of (1878), 108
Bicycles, 172–3, *172–3*
'Bills of Mortality', 180
  see also Medicine
Birmingham, 136
  Political Union, 40
'Black Country', *100–1*
'Bobbies', 36
Boers, colonies, 213, 214
  'Great Trek' (1836), 212

resent abolition of slavery, 47, 212
  war with Britain, 214, *215*, 216
Bonaparte, Joseph (1768–1844), 21
Bonaparte, Napoleon (1769–1821),
  18
  Berlin Decrees issued by, 21
  Consul, 18
  death, 26
  defeats royalist rising in Toulon,
  11
  Emperor, 18
  final defeat of, 25
  first exile, 23–4
  Hundred Days, 25
  origins of, 18
  Peninsular War, 21–2
  rise of, 18
  Russian campaign, 22–3
  second exile, 26
  war with Britain, 18–26
Bonny River, 209–10
Booth, Charles (1840–1916), 116
Bordeini Bey, 111
Borodino, Battle of (1812), 22–3
  see also Bonaparte, Napoleon
Botany Bay, 198, *198*
Bow Street Runners, 36
Boycott, Captain Charles (1832–97),
  131, *131*
Boyne, Battle of the (1690), 125
  see also Ireland
Bradshaw, George (1801–53), 92
Braxfield, Lord, Robert Macqueen
  (1722–99), 11
Brian Boru (926–1014), 133
Bright, John (1811–89), 68, 71, 80
Brisbane, *see* Australia
British Empire, 194, 216
  see also Africa; Australia;
  Canada; India; New Zealand
Brunel, Isambard Kingdom
  (1806–59), 31, 89
Burne-Jones, Sir Edward (1833–98),
  146, *147*
Buses, *144*

Camperdown, Battle of (1797), 19
Canada, 194–7, *195–7*, 201–2
  stamp, *217*
Canning, George (1770–1827), 30
Canton, bombardment of (1856),
  81–2
  European factories in, *81*
Caroline, Queen (1768–1821), 60
Cartwright, Mr, 13–14
Castlereagh, Viscount Robert
  Stewart (1769–1822), 28–30, 35
Chadwick, Sir Edwin (1800–90),
  55–8
Chartists (1838–48), 62–7, *64–7*
  results of, 67
Children, home life of, 153
  chimney sweeps, 106, *122*
  in factories, 12, 48–51, *48*
  in mines, *50*
  poverty and, *12, 116*
  in prison, *51*
China, 81–2
Cholera outbreak (1831), 140
  see also Diseases; Medicine
Clarkson, Thomas (1760–1846),
  45, 46
Clive, Baron Robert (1725–74), 206
Coach travel, 84, *84, 85*
Coal, children mining, *50*
  transported by steam, 85
Cobbett, William (1763–1835), 32,
  32, 37–8, 42, 50
Cobden, Richard (1804–65), 68
Cochrane, Admiral, Sir Alexander
  (1758–1832), 30
Collingwood, Baron Cuthbert
  (1750–1810), 16
Combination laws (1799, 1800), 13,
  35
Conservatives, 72
  see also Disraeli; Tories
Cook, Captain James (1728–79),
  181, 198
Cooper, Thomas (1805–92), *63, 65*
Copenhagen, Battle of (1802), 19
Corn Laws, repeal of (1846), 68–71,
  114, 128
Corn prices, 35
Cotton gin, invention of, 12
Crafts, 148, 157–8
Cricket, 152

Crime, 36
Crimean War, 75–80, *76–80, 83*
Cromwell, Oliver (1599–1658), 125
Crook, Mr, 117
Crossing-sweepers, *144*
Cruickshank, George (1792–1878),
  56
Crystal Palace, 96–8

Daguerre, Louis (1789–1851), 170,
  170
Dalhousie, Sir James Ramsay,
  Marquis (1812–60), 205
Das Kapital, 73
Darwin, Charles (1809–82), 160–2,
  160–2, 187
Darwin, Erasmus (1731–1802), 161
Davies, Emily (1830–1921), 153
Davitt, Michael (1846–1906), 131
Dickens, Charles (1812–70), *David
  Copperfield*, 200
  deathbed scenes, 180
  Great Expectations, 200
  Martin Chuzzlewit, 150, *185*
  on nurses, 185, *185*
  Oliver Twist, 56, *56*
  publishing methods, 150
Diseases, 180–2, *183*
  see also Cholera; Medicine
Disraeli, Benjamin (1804–81), *103,
  104, 106, 107, 108*
  attacks Peel on Corn Laws, 70
  character, 103
  foreign policy, 108
  marriage, 104
  in office for six years (1874–80),
  105–9
  origins, 103
  relations with Queen Victoria, 104
Dockers, conditions among, 117–20,
  118–20
Doctors, 180–3
Drainage systems, 137–9

East India Company, 203–6
Education, need for, 174
  State, 176
  Technical, 178–9
  see also Schools; Technical
  Colleges
Edward VII (1841–1910), 62, 83

Egypt, British army of occupation
  in, 110
  rebellion in (1882), 109
Elba, Napoleon on, 24
Electricity, see Lighting
Eliot, George (1819–80),
  Middlemarch, 181
Entertainments, 148, *148*

Factory Act (1833), 48–51
  (1847), 95
Faraday, Michael (1791–1867), 187
Farming, during French wars, 14
  golden age of (1850–80), 114, 156
Fashions, *149*
Fashoda, 112
Fenians, 130
Finland, conquered by Napoleon, 21
Fitzgerald, Lord Edward (1763–98),
  126
Fitzherbert, Maria (1756–1837), 60
Football, 151–2, *152*
Fox-Talbot, William Henry
  (1800–77), 170
France, Britain at war with
  (1793–1815), 10–12, 17–26
  in Morocco, 112
  plans for invasion of England
  (1803), 27
  richness and poverty of, 6
  States General, 6–7
  see also French Revolution;
  Bonaparte, Napoleon
Free trade, 68, 69
French Revolution, 6–10
  Bastille, fall of, *7, 8*
  Guillotine, *10*
  National Assembly, *8*
  republican colours, *9*
Friendly Societies, 53
  see also Trade Unions
Frost, John (d. 1877), 66

Gaelic, 133–4, *134*
'Gagging Acts', 35
Gas, see Lighting
George III (1738–1820), 60, *60*, 127
George IV (1762–1830), 60, *60*
Ghana, 210
Gladstone, William Ewart
  (1809–98), *102*

and *Alabama* compensation claim,
105
character, 102
Irish policy, 130–1, 132
joins Liberals, 72
marriage, 102
origins, 102
relations with Queen Victoria,
102–3
second ministry (1880–85), 109
and Sudan, 111–12
Goldsmith, Oliver (1728–74), 133
Gordon, General Charles George
(1833–85), 110–12
Goya, Francisco (1746–1828), *21, 22*
Grand National Consolidated
Trades Union (1834), 53–4
Great Exhibition (1851), 96–8, *96–8*
Great Mogul, 204, 206
Grey, Lord Charles (1764–1845),
38–9

Hardie, Keir (1856–1915), 121–2, *121*
Hay, Robert (1789–1847), 14–15
Haynau, General Julius
(1786–1853), 74, *74*
Hickman, Dr, 187
'Hobby horse', *172*
Holmes, Oliver Wendell (1809–94),
187
Holy Alliance (1815), 28–9
Home Rule, 132
Hospitals, conditions in, 183–6,
184, 186, 187, 191, 193
see also Medicine
Housing, 138–42
Howe, Admiral Richard (1726–99),
11, 16–17
Hudson, George (1800–71), *88*
Hudson, W. H. (1841–1922), 157
'Hundred Days', *see* Bonaparte,
Napoleon
Hunt, William Holman (1827–
1910), 146
Huskisson, William (1770–1830),
35, 38

Independent Labour Party, 120–2
India, 203–7, *203, 204*
caste system, 206
Mutiny (1857), 206–7, *207*

Queen Victoria, Empress of, 105–6
Sepoys, 204, 206
stamp, *217*
see also East India Company
Indians, Canadian, *197*, 201–2
Ireland, Act of Union (1800), 127
attempts to colonize, 124–6
Fenians, 130
Gaelic revival, 133–4, *134*
Home Rule, 132
housing contrasts, *126, 127*
Irish Republican Brotherhood,
see Fenians
Land Act (1870), 130
Land League, 130–1, 132
potato famines (1845, 1846), 68,
128, *128, 129*
rebellion (1798), 20
religion, 124–6, 127
Royal Irish Constabulary, 132
United Irishmen Society formed,
126

James I (1566–1625), 124
Jameson, Captain Leander (1853–
1917), 214
Jenner, Dr Edward (1749–1823),
181

Kemble, Fanny (1809–93), 88
Kenya, 210
Khartoum, 110–12
Kingsley, Mary (1862–1900), 209
Kruger, President S. J. P. (1825–
1904), 214

Labour Party, 122
Laennec, Rene (1781–1826), 182–3
Lamarck, Jean (1744–1829), 161
Leipzig, Battle of (1813), 24
Liberals, 72
see also Gladstone, W. E.
Liberal Unionists, 132
see also Ireland
Licensing Act (1872), 105
Light Brigade, Charge of the, *79*
see Balaclava
Lighting, 168–9, *168–9*
Limited Liability Act (1855), 109
Lister, Joseph, Baron (1827–1912),
189–91, *190, 192*

Literature, Victorian, 149–50
Liverpool, Lord (1770–1828), 30
Livingstone, David (1813–73), 211,
211
Lobengula, Chief (1833?–94), 214
London Workingmen's Association,
62–3
Louis XV, King of France
(1710–74), 7
Louis XVI, King of France
(1754–93), 6–8, *6*, 10, *10*
Loveless, George, 53
Lovett, William (1800–77), 63, *63*,
65–6
Ludd, Ned, *see* Luddite Movement
Luddite Movement, 13–14, *13*
Luxury, 114, *115*

Machinery, and the working
population, 12–13
Mafeking, relief of (1899–1900),
214
Mahdi, the, 110–12
Mann, Tom (1856–1941), 117
Manning, Cardinal Henry
(1808–92), 118, 120
Marie Antoinette, Queen of France
(1755–93), 8, 10, *11*
Martello towers, 20
Marx, Karl (1818–83), 73
Medical Officers of Health,
appointment of, 140
Medicine, 180–92
anaesthetics, 187–8, *188–90*
antiseptics, 189–92
apothecaries, 180
doctors, 180–3
lunatic asylums, *180*
nurses, 180, *185, 186*
operations, 187, *187–90*
physicians, 181
stethoscope, 182
surgeons, 181, 187
thermometer, 182
vaccination, 181–2, *182*
see also Hospitals
Melbourne, *see* Australia
**Melbourne, William Lamb, 2nd
Viscount (1779–1848), 61–2**
Metternich, Prince Klemens von
(1773–1859), 28, 29

Millais, Sir John Everett (1829–96), 146, *146*, 147
Mirabeau, Count Gabriel (1749–91), 8
Moore, Sir John (1761–1809), 21
Morocco, 112
Morse Code, 166, *166*
Moscow, Napoleon in, 23
Municipal Corporations Act (1835), 140

Napier, General Sir Charles (1782–1853), 65
Natal, 213
'Navvies', 90–1, *91*
  see also Railways
Navy, conditions in, 14–17, *17*
  press gangs, 14, *15*
Nelson, Admiral Horatio (1758–1805), 16
  character, 16
  death, *20*, 21
  at Trafalgar, 20
Newton, John (1725–1807), 45, 47
New Zealand, 200
  Maoris, 202, *202*
  sheep-shearing, *200*
  war canoe, *201*
Ney, Marshal Michel (1769–1815), 24–5
Nigeria, *209*, 210
Nightingale, Florence (1820–1910), 77
  in Crimean War, 77–8, 80, *80*
  early life, 77–8, 153
  on germs, 190
  at St Thomas's Hospital, 80, 186, *193*
Nile, Battle of the (1798), 18, 19
Nottingham Castle, *39*
Nurses, 180, *185*, *186*

O'Connor, Feargus (1796–1855), 65–6
Old Sarum, *39*
Oliver (spy), 33
Omdurman, Battle of (1898), 112, *112*
'Orator Hunt', Henry (1773–1835), 34
Origin of Species, The, 162

Owen, Robert (1771–1858), 48, 52

Painting, 146, 148
Palmerston, Lord Henry (1784–1865), 72–4, 80–1
Parliament, reform of, 36–40, *37–9*
Parnell, Charles Stewart (1846–91), 131, *132*
Pasteur, Louis (1822–95), 189–91, *192*
Paxton, Sir Joseph (1801–65), 96
Peel, Sir Robert (1788–1850), and Corn Laws, 68–70, 128
  death, 70
  and Penal code, 36
  Punch's memorial to, *70*
  and Queen Victoria, 62
'Peelers', 36, *36*
Penal code, 36
Peninsular War (1808–14), 21–2
Perkin, Sir William (1838–1907), 173
'Peterloo, massacre of', 34–5, *34*
Phillip, Arthur (1738–1814), 198–9
Photography, 170–1, *170–1*
Pictures, 146, 148
Piece-work, 116, *117*
Pitt, William (1759–1806), 9–11
  death, 21
  and Irish problem, 126–7
  war policies, 11, 19
Place, Francis (1771–1854), 35
Plassey, Battle of (1757), 206
Plimsoll, Samuel (1824–98), 106, 108
Police, formation of, 36
Political Register, 32
Poor Law (1835), 54–7, 65
Population, 136
Portugal, Napoleon invades, 21
Postage stamps, *62*, *217*
Potter, Beatrice, Mrs Sidney Webb (1858–1943), 116
Poverty, 12, *12*, 55–7, *115–17*, *138*, *139*
  see also Children; Dockers; Piece-work; Poor Law; Slums; Towns; Trade Unions; Workhouse
Pre-Raphaelites, 146, 148
Press gangs, 14, *15*
Priestley, Dr Joseph (1733–1804), 10, 187

Prussia, war with France (1792–7), 9–11
Public Health Act (1848), 140

Quakers, 45

Raglan, James Somerset, Baron (1788–1855), 76
Railways, *86–95*, 165
  benefits from, 92–3, 95
  boom in (1838–48), 88
  broad gauge, 89
  first (1830), 85–8
  first timetable, 92
  making the, 89–91
Reform Act (1867), 104
Reform Bill (1832), 38–40
Reibey, Mary, 200
Rhodes, Cecil (1853–1902), 213–14
Rhodesia, 214
'Rotten boroughs', *see* Parliament, reform of
Royal Geographical Society, 211
Russell, William Howard (1821–1907), 77, *77*
Russia, alliance with France, 112
  forces Turkey to set up state of Bulgaria, 108
  Napoleon invades, 22–3, *23*
  negotiates with Napoleon, 21
  see also Crimean War

Sadler, Michael Thomas (1780–1835), 49
St Helena, Napoleon exiled to, 26
Salisbury, Lord Robert (1830–1903), 112
Schools, 174, *175*, *177*
  Education Act (1870), 176
  Lancastrian, 174–5, *175*
  see also Technical Colleges
Science, 160–2
Scutari, 77, *80*
  see also Crimean War
Sebastopol, *79*
  see also Crimean War
Secret Ballot Act (1872), 104, *105*
Self Help, see Smiles, Samuel
Sepoys, 204, 206
Sewing machines, 173

Shaftesbury, Anthony Ashley Cooper, Earl (1801–85), fights for factory children, 49, *49, 139*
views on Sunday observance, 151
Shaw, George Bernard (1856–1950), *135*
Shelley, Percy Bysshe (1792–1822), 30
Sheridan, Richard Brinsley (1751–1816), 133
Sidmouth, Henry Addington, Viscount (1757–1844), 33, 35
Simpson, Sir James Young (1811–70), 187–8, *188*
Slavery, abolition of, 42–7
auctions, 43
in Cape Colony, 47
irons, *45*
'middle passage', 42–4, *44*
ships, *44*
in West Indies, *42*, 44–7
Slums, 138–40, *138*
Smiles, Samuel (1812–1904), 102
South Africa, 212–16
Spain, Napoleon invades, 21, *22*
Speenhamland, Berkshire, 55
Spithead, mutiny at (1797), 16, 18
Sport, 151–2, *152*
Stanley, Sir H. M. (1841–1904), 211
Steam engines, 85, *86*, 165
see also Railways
Steel, *163*, 173
Stephenson, George (1781–1848), 85–7
Streets, *143, 144,* 145, *145*
Strikes, *see* Trade Unions
Sudan, 110–12
Suez Canal, opening of, *107*, 165
purchase of, 106, *107*
Sundays, life on, 150–1, *150–1*
Sweeps, 106, *122*

Taff Vale Railway, 122
Tawell, John, 166
Taxes, 31–2, *31*
Technical colleges, 174, 178–9, *178*
Telegraphy, 165–6, *165*
Tel-el-Kebir, Battle of (1882), 110
Telephone, 166–7, *167*
Tennis, 151, *152*

Tennyson, Alfred Lord (1809–92), 153
Tillett, Ben (1860–1943), 117–18
Tilsit, Treaty of (1807), 21
Tolpuddle, Dorset, 53, *54*
see also Trade Unions
Tone, Wolfe (1763–98), 126
Tories, and reform, 38–40
and Trade Unions, 53
see also Conservatives; Trade Unions
Towns, growth of the, 136–9, *136–9*
Trade Unions, early attempts to form, 13, 35, *52*
Grand National Consolidated Trades Union (1834), 53–4
new model formed (1851), 113
and picketing law, 108
registered as Friendly Societies, 105
see also Dockers
Trafalgar, Battle of (1805), 19–21
Traffic, *see* Streets
Transport, *164,* 165
see also Bicycles; Railways
Transport and General Workers' Union, 120
Transvaal, 47, *212,* 213
Treves, Sir Frederick (1853–1923), 188
Trollope, Frances (1780–1863), *12*
Turkey, defeated by Russia (1877), 108
Typewriters, 173

Unionist Party, *see* Liberal Unionists
United Irishmen, 126
Utilitarians, 32

Vaccination, 181–2, *182*
Versailles, France, 7–8
Victoria, Queen (1819–1901), *61*
birthday, 61
claims right to interfere in foreign policy, 72
court life, 62, 83
death, 216
and Disraeli, 104
as Empress of India, 105–6
family life, 62

and Gladstone, 102–3
interest in the telephone, 167
marriage, 62
and Palmerston, 72–4
receives chloroform in childbirth, 188
retires into mourning for Albert, 83
unpopularity of, 62
as a young queen, 61–2
Victory, H.M.S., 17
see also Nelson
Vienna, Congress of (1814), 28
Village life, 154–8, *154–6*

Waterloo, Battle of (1815), *24–5,* 25–6
Watt, James (1736–1819), 14, 163
Webb, Mrs Sidney (1858–1943), 116
Wellesley, Sir Arthur, *see* Wellington, Duke of
Wellington, Arthur Wellesley, 1st Duke of (1769–1852), *21*
defeats Napoleon at Waterloo, 25–6
drives French from Spain, 21–2
opposes railways, 86–7, 88
as Prime Minister, 38
and reform, 38–40
report on Ireland sent to, 128
Whigs, growing unpopularity of, 58
and penal reform, 37–40
and slavery, 46–7
and Trade Unions, 53
see also Liberals
Whitbread, Samuel (1758–1815), 46
Wilberforce, William (1759–1833), 45–7, *47*
Willans, Mr, 33–4
William III (1650–1702), 125
William IV (1765–1837), 38, 39, 60
Wolseley, Sir Garnet (1833–1913), 110
Women, growing freedom of, 153–4
Workhouses, 56

Yeats, William Butler (1865–1939), *135*

Zulus, *212,* 213

Acknowledgements

Aerofilms Limited : 37, 151, 171
Ashmolean Museum, Department of Eastern Art, Oxford : 204
British Museum : 18, 21, 60, 62, 208, 209, 217
National Film Board of Canada : 196
Musée Carnavalet, Paris : 7
Coda Music Company © 1965, *The wearing of the green,* arranged and adapted by Finton Connolly: 135
Greater London Council : 176, 177
Imperial War Museum : 76
André Jammes, photographer : 81
Mansell Collection : 6, 8, 9, 10, 11, 13, 17, 23, 24/5, 36, 38, 50, 54, 55, 57, 63, 66, 67, 77, 79, 80, 81, 84, 86, 87, 88, 95, 100/101, 107, 111, 112, 113, 118/19, 120, 126, 127, 129, 136, 146, 147, 149, 152, 157, 162, 167, 169, 192, 200, 207, 215
National Maritime Museum, Greenwich : 15, 17, 20, 161
National Portrait Gallery : 32, 46, 47, 49, 102, 108, 135, 160
Punch : 70, 106, 107, 117, 144
Radio Times Hulton Picture Library : 39, 78, 90, 96, 121, 128, 142, 148, 150, 156, 166, 178, 183, 199, 215

Museum of English Rural Life, University of Reading : 154
Science Museum London : 170
Science Museum London, Crown Copyright : 170
Sheffield City Libraries : 137
South Africa House : 213
Board of Governors of St Thomas's Hospital : 186, 187
The Times Publishing Co. Ltd : 77
Alexander Turnbull Library : 200
Université de Paris à la Sorbonne : 192
Victoria and Albert Museum, Crown Copyright : 94, 98, 145, 203
The Wellcome Trust : 139, 182, 188, 189, 190, 191
Wilberforce House, Hull : 43, 44
Workers' Music Association : 99, 123

MAPS AND DIAGRAMS

Penguin Education Art Department : 19, 29, 44, 59, 72, 75, 89, 99, 110, 123, 124, 125, 135, 159, 165, 169, 194, 197, 201, 205, 210, 213